WaldenUniversity

College of Management and Technology

This is to certify that the doctoral study by

Qais Alfaraj

has been found to be complete and satisfactory in all respects,
and that any and all revisions required by
the review committee have been made.

Review Committee
Dr. Carol-Anne Faint, Committee Chairperson, Doctor of Business Administration Faculty

Dr. Bethany Mickahail, Committee Member, Doctor of Business Administration Faculty

Dr. Krista Laursen, University Reviewer, Doctor of Business Administration Faculty

Chief Academic Officer
Eric Riedel, Ph.D.

Walden University
2019

Abstract

Attaining and Sustaining Competitive Advantage in Dubai's Real Estate Industry

by

Qais Alfaraj

MBA, Kuwait University, 2004

BA, Kuwait University, 1999

Doctoral Study Submitted in Partial Fulfillment

of the Requirements for the Degree of Doctor of

Business Administration

Walden University

April 2019

Abstract

Real estate business leaders who fail to attain and sustain competitive advantage to increase profitability during periods of unstable or declining markets, experience either lost profits or bankruptcy. In Dubai, United Arab Emirates, the brokerage market is saturated with over 5,000 active brokers and more than 2,000 registered real estate offices. The purpose of this multiple case study was to explore the strategies that successful leaders of Dubai medium-sized real estate businesses implemented to attain and sustain competitive advantage to increase profitability during periods of unstable or declining markets. The population for the study included business leaders of 4 medium-sized real estate businesses in Dubai, who had successfully implemented competitive advantage strategies. Data were collected from semistructured interviews with the 4 leaders and from artifacts such as the company websites and social media pages. The conceptual framework for this study was the strength-weakness-opportunity-threat analysis technique. Inductive analysis was used to code and identify themes in the collected data, and the trustworthiness of interpretations was supported by member checking. Four themes emerged: reduce operating costs, execute corporate real estate management, promote corporate social responsibility, and utilize human capital. Findings from this study could contribute to positive social change by providing real estate business leaders with insights regarding strategy implementations necessary for attaining and sustaining competitive advantage and increasing financial independence, thereby promoting the culture and strengthening the local economy.

Attaining and Sustaining Competitive Advantage in Dubai's Real Estate Industry

by

Qais Alfaraj

MBA, Kuwait University, 2004

BA, Kuwait University, 1999

Doctoral Study Submitted in Partial Fulfillment

of the Requirements for the Degree of Doctor of

Business Administration

Walden University

April 2019

Dedication

I dedicate this doctoral study to my wife Dina, my two lovely girls Fay and Bibi

for their prayers, love, and support during this doctoral journey.

Acknowledgments

I would like to thank Dr. Carol-Anne Faint, Dr. Bethany Mickahail, Dr. Krista Laursen, and my other instructors and classmates at Walden University for your tremendous support. Your mentorship and guidance significantly contributed to my success.

Table of Contents

i

List of Tables

Section 1: Foundation of the Study

Strategic management is a process to determine the internal (strengths and weaknesses) and external (opportunities and threats) factors impacting the formulation of strategies to attain and sustain competitive advantage (Dyer, Godfrey, Jensen, & Bryce, 2016). Competitive advantage pertains to the performance of a business that includes high relative profitability, above average returns, benefit-cost gap, superior financial performance, economic profits, positive differential profits in excess of opportunity costs, and cross-sectional differential in the spread between product market demand and marginal cost (Sigalas, 2015). However, competition continuously grows in different industries either locally or globally. The global financial crisis affected the main economic source for Dubai, United Arab Emirates (UAE): the oil and gas industry. The real estate sector and other industries played an invaluable role in the recovery of Dubai's economy. However, the number of real estate agencies outpaced the supply of listings which resulted in a tight competition in the market and lead to bankruptcy for many companies. My objective in this study was to explore the strategies real estate business leaders implement to attain and sustain competitive advantage to increase profitability during periods of unstable or declining markets.

Background of the Problem

The American market leads the world in real estate transactions, with approximately $540 billion in 2016. The Asia Pacific follows in the rankings with roughly $448 billion of investments in the market. Europe, Africa, and the Middle East are still recovering from a decline with a real estate transaction value of $347 billion

(Siemińska & Krajewska, 2017). The UAE is an oil-dependent country, with oil and gas

as the main economic product. The global financial crisis led to a drop in oil prices that

indicated a rough market sentiment and affected the gross domestic product (GDP) rate

(Daleure, 2016). However, the real estate sector strengthens the economy through the fall

of rents and house prices in order to produce large projects in 2017 and continuously

increase housing supply in 2018. During the crisis period from 2008 to 2012, the oil

sector contributed 31.58% of UAE's GDP, while the non-oil sector provided 68.42%

divided by different industries with the highest contribution from the real estate sector

with an increase of 18% from 2009 to 2012 (Ahmed, 2015). The GDP of UAE reached

the lowest point in 2017, with 1.7% coming from an average of 4.1% from 2012 to 2016

and an expected growth of 3.4% from 2018 to 2020 (Oxford Business Group, 2018). In

this study, I explored how to attain and sustain competitive advantage in the real estate

industry, which is one of the highest contributors to the Dubai's economy aside from the

oil sector. The study was needed because of the growing competition in the real estate

market along with a global financial crisis.

Problem Statement

The drop in oil prices in the UAE resulting from a global financial crisis,

negatively impacted key markets; consequently, real estate agency owners experienced

declining demand in terms of residential performance, rentals, and volumes of the

property transactions (Wiedmann, Salama, & Ibrahim, 2016). Between the fourth quarter

of 2016 and third quarter of 2017, the average sales prices for Dubai's residential

property declined approximately 2% and an estimated 7% decline in rents along with the biggest challenge for the real estate industry is the 5% value added tax effective in 2018 (Al Faris & Soto, 2016; Deloitte, 2018). The general business problem is that some business owners fail to operate companies within an unstable market, impacted by lower margins, and higher business cost factors. The specific business problem is that some owners in Dubai's real estate industry lack strategies to attain and sustain competitive advantage to increase profitability during periods of unstable or declining markets.

Purpose Statement

The purpose of this qualitative multiple case study was to explore the strategies Dubai real estate business leaders use to attain and sustain competitive advantage to increase profitability during periods of unstable or declining markets. The study population consisted of four real estate business leaders in the regions of Dubai, an emirate that has demonstrated success within the UAE and the Middle East. Interviewees were active and licensed brokers, participating in both off plan and ready units, handling both residential and commercial properties, and working within both sales and lease markets. The study's implications for positive social change include the potential to establish economic growth within the industry, potentially adding value to larger communities by stabilizing markets, strengthening the local economy, and potentially improving families' lifestyles. In addition, investors or expatriates may make investments in the real estate sector that could promote the unique culture and society of the UAE.

Nature of the Study

I selected a qualitative research method for the study. A qualitative researcher uses narrative dialogues to understand decision-making processes and comprehend the aspect of social life through the experience and attitudes of the subject (McCusker & Gunaydin, 2015; Saunders, Lewis, & Thornhill, 2015). Therefore, the qualitative methodology was the most appropriate for this study because of the explorative nature of the research question (Marshall & Rossman, 2016). A mixed methods researcher applies both qualitative and quantitative methods relying upon interview and statistical analyses (Makrakis & Kostoulas-Makrakis, 2016; Morse, 2017). A quantitative researcher examines the relationships between variables through numerical, statistical and graphical techniques (Antonakis, Bastardoz, Liu, & Schriesheim, 2014; Griga, 2017). I did not select a mixed method approach because I did not include statistical analysis of variables' relationships or differences. A quantitative approach was not appropriate as I was not seeking to model explanations of behavior.

I selected a multiple case study design for this study. A multiple case study involves interviewing participants from a group of businesses to understand decision-making processes and the various strategies applied to increase profitability (Yin, 2014). A multiple case study was appropriate because I determined that insights may arise from explorations of multiple agencies to enhance the richness of the investigation. The single case is commonly used on a critical, extreme, or unique case (Saunders et al., 2015). The single case study was not appropriate for the study because the intent was to explore more than one case or organization to understand the phenomenon. The phenomenological researcher (Moustakas, 1994) explores the meanings of real-life context of the participants. Thus, phenomenological was inappropriate because my intent was not to explore meanings of participants' lived experiences related to phenomenon.

Research Question

What strategies do Dubai real estate business leaders use to attain and sustain competitive advantage to increase profitability during periods of unstable or declining markets?

Interview Questions

1. How does strategic management or planning help you create and develop competitive advantage?

2. How do your strategies and business plans address the opportunities and threats pertaining to the changing economy and real estate industry of Dubai?

3. How does innovation contribute on attaining and sustaining competitive advantage?

4. What are the strategies you are generating as the UAE imposes a tax on 2018 affecting the real estate market?

5. How are you handling the current decline of Dubai's real estate sector with a falling rental and sales prices?

6. What additional information can you provide to help me understand strategies your organization uses to attain and sustain competitive advantage in changing real estate markets in Dubai?

Conceptual Framework

I selected the study strengths, weaknesses, opportunities and threats (SWOT) analysis technique as the conceptual framework. Albert Humphrey developed the SWOT analysis in the year 1960 while working for the Stanford Research Institute, now known as SRI International (Humphrey, 2005; Solberg Søilen, 2015). Humphrey, an American business and management consultant, whose expertise included organizational management and cultural change (Gurel, 2017). The SWOT analysis is a strategic planning method for evaluating four tenets of a business: (a) strengths, (b) weaknesses, (c) opportunities, and (d) threats (Menga, Dan, Lu, & Liu, 2015). The internal factors are considered the strengths and weaknesses of a business that include the customer, employees, capabilities, resources, and processes (Czajkowska, 2016). Conversely, opportunities and threats are classified as the external factors that involve the environment, industry, economy, future trends, demographics, geographical considerations, and technology (Chen, 2014). Businesses use the SWOT framework as an effective tool for identifying potential risks and opportunities impacting a business when strategic enhancements generate increased profits compared to competitors in the market (Dyer et al., 2016). I used the SWOT framework as a lens to explore the strategies participants used to increase competitive advantage.

Operational Definitions

I offer the following operational definitions to assist readers in comprehending the meaning of some specialized terms I use throughout the study.

Absorptive capacity: Absorptive capacity is the ability to acquire, assimilate, transform, and exploit knowledge into dynamic organizational and operational capabilities (Lau & Lo, 2015).

Competitive advantage: Competitive advantage is when a firm produces higher profits in the market over the competitors (Dyer et al., 2016).

Dynamic capabilities: Dynamic capabilities are procedures, processes, and routines that continuously expand existing resources and improve operating capabilities (Dyer et al., 2016).

Human capital: Human capital comprises the skills, knowledge, and professional competencies of the employees of a firm, and a combination of genetic inheritance, education and experience (Todericiu & Stanit, 2015).

Intellectual capital: Intellectual capital refers to the human and organizational resources, know-how, and technical knowledge capacity of a firm (Todericiu & Stanit, 2015).

Real options reasoning: Real options reasoning is a dynamic framework to modify tangible and intangible resources towards the diversity of the market, technology, and environment (Jahanshahi et al., 2015).

Resource-based view: Resource-based view refers to the firm's capabilities and resources such as the physical, financial, human, tangible, and intangible assets in creating strategies (Balashova & Gromova, 2016).

Service innovation: Service innovation is the creation of new service features, processes, technologies, and methods using all the tangible and intangible factors (Lusch & Nambisan, 2015).

Social capital: Social capital is a connection and relationship between a firm and the society through a shared set of values that also influences collective learning, absorptive capacity, and competitive advantage (Chuang, Chen, & Lin, 2016).

Strategic management: Strategic management is a strategy used as a source of competitive advantage through competitive/market forces, resource-based view, dynamic capabilities, and relational view (Eloranta & Turunen, 2015).

Assumptions, Limitations, and Delimitations

Assumptions

An assumption is a statement that is presumed to be true for a specific purpose like building a theory (Wargo, 2015). I made two assumptions in my study. First, I assumed the interview participants had sufficient knowledge of their organizations' practices and strategies. Second, I assumed that participants responded to the interview questions truthfully and honestly.

Limitations

Limitations are areas that are beyond the control of the researcher (Wargo, 2015). I identified two potential limitations in this study. First, there may have been some biases in the participants' responses. Second, because I limited the size of the study population, the findings may not be generalizable to other businesses.

Delimitations

Delimitations are the boundaries set for a study (Nelms, 2015). The delimitations of the study include the sizes of the organization, the geographic location of the study, and the sector of the industry. First, I only included medium size real estate companies that employs fewer than 500 employees. Second, the companies are located in Dubai, UAE. Third, I only focused on the real estate industry because the purpose of the study was to explore strategies real estate business leaders use to attain and sustain competitive advantage to increase profitability during periods of unstable or declining markets.

Significance of the Study

My findings may contribute to business practice by showing ways to mitigate economic impacts on the real estate markets in Dubai and identifying strategies to support business growth in preparation for UAE's World Expo in 2020. Thus, business growth may encourage home and property sales stimulating expansions in the real estate industry (Daleure, 2016). Through the concept and sources of competitive advantage, real estate business leaders may increase profitability during period of unstable or declining markets.

Contribution to Business Practice

The findings from the study could have significance for real estate business leaders looking to attain and sustain competitive advantage during a global financial crisis. The findings may provide specific strategies that may help business leaders to improve profitability, performance, or sustainability. Entrepreneurs may create competitive advantage strategies for exploiting opportunities through the resources and capabilities of their firms as well as the industry itself (Ngah, Abd Wahab, & Saleh, 2015).

Implications for Social Change

My findings may effect social change through not only the financial stability of real estate firms, but also social, economic and environmental sustainability (Alawadi, 2017). Competitive advantage may create jobs and financial independence for individuals and families, as well as providing beneficial investments for real estate investors. With investments into Dubai society, individuals and families might experience improved quality of life and opportunities for social and cultural engagement.

A Review of the Professional and Academic Literature

The purpose of this multiple case study was to explore the strategies Dubai real estate business leaders use to attain and sustain competitive advantage to increase profitability during periods of unstable or declining markets. Eloranta and Turunen (2015) analyzed competitive advantage through strategic management theories, competitive forces, the resource-based view, dynamic capabilities, and the relational view. Dyer et al. (2016) studied the flow of strategic management process to achieve competitive advantage is through identifying the internal (strengths and weaknesses) and external (opportunities and threats) factors in formulating strategies.

In this literature review section, I offer a general background on previous studies regarding strategic management and innovation towards competitive advantage. The purpose of the literature review is to provide the reader with overall knowledge about the subject of attaining and sustaining competitive advantage. I have organized the literature review into subsections on (a) competitive advantage, (b) strategic management, (c) strengths and weaknesses, (d) opportunities and threats, and (e) innovation.

A significant portion of the information in the literature review was drawn from academic peer-reviewed journal articles. The primary search terms I used to gather this information from academic databases were *competitive advantage, strategic management, innovation, SWOT, property investors, developers*, and *real estate strategies*. I searched for these terms using Google Scholar, Walden University Library, and variety of business and management databases such as Research Gate, Emerald Management, SAGE, ScienceDirect, ProQuest Central, Springer, Crossref Metadata Search, and Business Source Complete. Of the 207 references, 182 (88%) were published within the last 5 years (2015 to 2019), and 88% of the total references are peer-reviewed. Therefore, these percentages comply with Walden University's DBA doctoral study rubric requirements. Table 1 includes a summary of the different totals and types of sources.

Table 1

Summary of Reference Types and Their Currency

Type	Older	2015	2016	2017	2018	2019	Total	Percentage
Peer- reviewed journal articles	21	92	42	20	5	0	180	86.97
Books	4	6	7	7	0	0	24	11.59
Others	0	1	0	1	1	0	3	1.46
Total	25	99	49	28	6	0	207	100

SWOT Analysis

The SWOT analysis is an excellent method that has come to be used as a standard in strategic planning. The SWOT evaluates four tenets of a business: (a) strengths, (b) weaknesses, (c) opportunities, and (d) threats (Menga et al., 2015). Abdel-Basset, Mohammed, and Smarandache (2018) considered SWOT as a decision-making tool to utilize in constructing strategies to enhance strengths, remove weaknesses, seize opportunities, and avoid threats. Albert Humphrey developed SWOT analysis in the year

1960 while working for the SRI International (Solberg Søilen, 2015). However, Humphrey denied inventing the method and explained that it originally came from a research project worked on with Marion Dosher, Dr. Otis Benepe, and Birger Lie. The SWOT's continuous growth and development are associated with Philip Selznick, Alfred DuPont Chandler, Kenneth Andrews, Harry Igor Ansoff, Heinz Weihrich, Richard Dealtry, Thomas Wheelen, and J. David Hunger (Gurel, 2017).

The SWOT analysis is an effective tool for identifying threats that could possibly convert into opportunities in creating or enhancing such strategies to achieve competitive advantage. Dyer et al. (2016) recognized that external analysis includes market or industry competition and customer analysis, while internal analysis consists of the resource-based view and capabilities of the firm as part of the strategic management process. Dyer et al. (2016) added that the customer analysis involves price sensitivity (consumer's willingness to purchase the product/service) and segmentation analysis (dividing customers based on similar needs or wants). Czajkowska (2016) identified the internal factors as the strengths and weaknesses of a business which includes the customer, employees, capabilities, resources, and processes. Conversely, Chen (2014) described opportunities and threats as the external factors involving the environment, industry, economy, future trends, demographics, geographical considerations, and technology.

The process of SWOT analysis is not limited to either a combination of strengths and weaknesses or opportunities and threats. According to Abdel-Basset et al. (2018), an organization can apply SWOT analysis in four strategic approaches:

strengths/opportunities (SO), using the opportunities through existing strengths; strengths/threats (ST), utilizing the strengths to eliminate or reduce the impact of threats; weaknesses/opportunities (WO), handling the weaknesses to acquire the benefits of opportunities; and weaknesses/threats (WT), pursuing to diminish the impact of threats by considering the weaknesses. Gurel (2017) classified the variables for organizational strengths and weaknesses are marketing, research and development, management information system, management team, operations, finance, and human resource while the environmental opportunities and threats comprise societal, governmental, economic, competitive, supplier, and market changes.

SWOT analysis has a disadvantage in the strategic decision-making process. Hence, researchers have integrated different approaches to developing a new variation of the analysis. Zivkovic et al. (2015) used SWOT analysis to define and prioritize possible development strategies for the technical faculty in Bor (TFB) of the University of Belgrade, Serbia. The researchers added the analytical network process (ANP) method to define the relationship between the goals, SWOT factors, SWOT sub-factors, and alternative or possible strategies in a hierarchical structure. With the ANP-SWOT method, the researchers found potential growth, development, and increase in the TFB's competitive position. Groselj and Zadnik Stirn (2015) also applied the combination of SWOT analysis and ANP which they named A'WOT. The researchers identified sustainable development as the most appropriate strategy for the environmental management problem of Pohorje, Slovenia through the A'WOT approach which contained the objective, strategic goals, SWOT factors, and the alternatives.

Researchers have proposed different methods to modify the possible weaknesses of SWOT analysis. Tavana et al. (2016) proposed a new hybrid method using an intuitionistic fuzzy (IF), analytic hierarchy process (AHP) and SWOT analysis to identify and evaluate the criteria and sub-criteria in outsourcing decision making. Using the IF-AHP model and SWOT analysis, the researchers found the high importance of improving the product quality with competitive conditions and increasing customer satisfaction as the core of a business. In contrast, Abdel-Basset et al. (2018) combined SWOT analysis with neutrosophic AHP model to interpret vague, inconsistent, and incomplete information that exists in the real world better than fuzzy or IF theories. The researchers noted the impact of N-AHP in evaluating and selecting efficient and effective strategies of Starbucks company.

Other researchers have noted shortcomings in the traditional SWOT approach, therefore, different strategies were associated to balance the SWOT technique. Zare, Mehri-Tekmeh, and Karimi (2015) combined SWOT analysis with AHP method and fuzzy technique for order performance by similarity to ideal solution (TOPSIS) for planning and decision-making in electricity supply chain. The researchers determined an action plan through the fuzzy-TOPSIS method, which defines the final weights of SWOT factors and prioritizing of strategies. The result was that governments shall support renewable energies and global networks in meeting electricity demands with eco-friendly procedures. Cayir Ervural et al. (2018) also used the SWOT analysis to identify criteria and sub-criteria, and integrated ANP to determine the weights of each of the SWOT factors and sub-factors, and applied TOPSIS to prioritize alternative strategies towards Turkey's energy planning.

The SWOT analysis was an appropriate framework for this study exploring the strategies Dubai real estate business leaders use to attain and sustain competitive advantage to increase profitability during periods of unstable or declining market. SWOT analysis contributed to the research study changing general perspective to solutions, learning the positive and negative impact of internal and external factors, and prepare strategic decisions. Furthermore, SWOT could fit to other theories such as Porter's five forces model that may promote group discussion and creative participatory technique, encourages current and future goals, and may be applicable to different analytical levels (Dyer et al., 2016; Gurel, 2017).

Alternative Theories

Porter's generic strategies. In the year 1980, Michael Porter developed the three generic management strategies inspired by the complexity of competition in different markets and industries. In Porter's original work, he identified four generic approaches and grouped into two axes, the target market and the type of advantage (Gould & Desjardins, 2015). Eventually, the strategy was divided into two levels: the corporate strategy, which aims for long-term goals of a firm; and the functional strategy, which refers to technique serving the goals of marketing, sales, productions, and finance (Salavou, 2015). Porter's became the most dominant framework for assessing competitive strategies within the strategic management literature among of his opponents were Miles and Snow, and Hofer and Schendel in 1978, Dess and Davis in 1987, and Parnell in 1997 (Salavou, 2015).

The first strategy is the cost leadership strategy, a business strategy establishing a competitive advantage through low cost operation. Porter (1980) described cost leadership as a method for cost minimization in areas such as the service, advertising, research and development, and environmental standards (Bayraktar, Hancerliogullari, Cetinguc, & Calisir, 2016). Cost leadership is a process of producing or distributing goods and services at a lower cost than the competitors within the industry, thus, reducing and controlling the costs to achieve sustainable competitive advantage (Pulaj, Kume, & Cipi, 2015). Cost leaders are cost-conscious or price-sensitive customers (Delmas & Pekovic, 2015). However, Porter suggested a cost leadership strategy is suitable for mature or stable environments (Prajogo, 2016).

The second strategy is the differentiation, an approach where firms create a unique identity for their products and services. Porter (1980) defined differentiation as an opportunity for firms to compete in the market or industry by prioritizing high quality products and services, creative and unique designs, establishing a brand image and loyalty, and facilitating innovation (Kaya, 2015). The strategy results in customers who are willing to pay higher prices due to the product or service differentiation (Zehir, Can, & Karaboga, 2015). Differentiators adapt more entrepreneurial activities than cost leaders, and have strong marketing skills, creative flair, product engineering and coordination between functional areas (Kaya, 2015). Contrary to cost leadership, differentiation is appropriate for a dynamic or growing environment (Prajogo, 2016).

The third strategy is the focus, a strategy that targets a niche market or audience. Porter (1980) identified focus strategy targeting a particular group of buyers, a segment of the product line, or geographic market. In combination with cost leadership, it reduces a variety of organizational problems (Wicker, Soebbing, Feiler, & Breuer, 2015). The focus strategy aims to serve the customers in a narrow market segment either through low cost or differentiation and generates higher profits (Pulaj et al., 2015). According to Dyer et al. (2016), Porter's generic strategies apply within constraints called five forces composed of new entrants (new firms joining the industry), supplier power (the ability to lower/raise the price, quality, and availability of the product), substitutes (fundamentally different but functions as the other product), buyer power (the ability to demand from suppliers), and rivalry (competition among firms within an industry).

Strategies may vary by the industry or market; some strategies might be applicable to a certain industry but not to another. According to Salavou (2015), the positive impact of Porter's (1980) generic strategies to various industries include electronics, crystal glass, clothing/manufacturing (Mahdi et al., 2015), construction (Kaiser, Arbi, & Ahlemann, 2015), and food sector (Mutunga & Minja, 2014). However, Porter's generic strategy was a possible alternative for this study because my intent was to explore competitive advantage strategies for the real estate industry. Nonetheless, SWOT analysis was most appropriate for the study because the framework is applicable to any industry and useful for exploring strategies to attain and sustain competitive advantage to increase profitability during periods of unstable or declining markets.

The 7 S model. The model provides a broad yet succinct way to capture the key strategic elements of an organization. Tom Peters, Robert Waterman, Julien Philips, Richard Pascale, and Anthony Athos of McKinsey consultants developed the 7 S model in the year 1980s (Ravanfar, 2015). The 7 dimensions are divided into two: (a) hard triangle; strategy, structure, and systems, and (b) soft square; style, staffing, skills, and shared value (Dyer et al., 2016). Organizations use the McKinsey 7 S framework to assess readiness (Aldairi, Khan, & Munive-Hernandez, 2016).

The hard triangle elements are easy to create alignment or realignment. Strategy is the most important element as it is the plan to achieve and sustain competitive advantage in the market; while, the structure which serves as the organizational chart of the firm; and the systems are the process and procedures to determine the activities of the business (Ravanfar, 2015). The soft square are the elements that are difficult to change and influence. Staffing is the human resource management process in the organization; skills pertain to the abilities of individuals including the organization; style refers to the type of leadership, commitment, and management; and shared values are the beliefs and norms shared within an organization (Teh & Corbitt, 2015).

The 7 S model is known to be effective in different ways. Dyer et al. (2016) enumerated adequate methods to achieve efficiency of the model (a) identify the current state of the organization and misalignments, (b) rank order misalignments based on the importance of the misalignment with strategy, (c) develop plans to create alignment, (d) understand how the proposed change affects other elements in the model, and (e) adjust plans accordingly. McKinsey 7 S framework is widely used in the field of Information

Technology (Aldairi et al., 2016). Hence, the 7 S model is also an alternative method for the study as the intent is to explore competitive advantage strategies for the real estate industry. Conversely, the SWOT analysis is appropriate for the study as the framework is applicable to any industry on exploring strategies to attain and sustain competitive advantage to increase profitability during periods of unstable or declining markets specifically in the real estate sector.

Real Estate Industry of Dubai

The UAE is a federal country with seven emirates named Ajman, Dubai, Fujairah, Ras Al Khaimah, Sharjah, Umm Al Quwain, and the capital, Abu Dhabi. Oil and gas are the main economic source of UAE and majorly produced by Abu Dhabi. However, Dubai started the different fields over the other emirates such as the tourism, trade, and investment, in particular, the real estate/property sector. The federal and local government allows not only the UAE nationals but also foreigners to invest and own real property (Jadalhaq, 2017). Foreigners possess the same rights as the nationals in terms of labor, health, education, public freedoms, housing and real estate ownership yet with certain conditions and agreements. Ibrahim (2018) classified the foreigners in two forms: (a) the natural foreigner person composes of relative, absolute, and preferential; and (b) the juristic foreigner person consists of simple, multinational, and transnational.

Real estate property ownership has certain rules and regulations to follow that includes the rights of locals and foreigners. Jadalhaq (2017) indicated that legal powers on real estate, including land, fixed building, or a unit in a building include using (living), exploiting (leasing), and disposing (demolish or sell). Ibrahim (2018) provided different types of ownership as per the United Kingdom law: (a) freehold, infinite ownership on

land and all buildings, the highest and strongest form; (b) leasehold, an agreement

between the tenant and landlord; and (c) common hold, equivalent to freehold ownership

of individual flats called condominium. Conversely, the UAE nationals pursued the

Sharia law pertaining to ownership or property rights of either the locals or foreigners as

follows: (a) usufruct right, a finite agreement to use and exploit the property of another

maintaining the original condition; (b) right of use and residence, only the agreed parties

have the rights to use and occupy; and (c) musataha right, the holder authorizes another

party to use and exploit the land, neither construct a building or invest in mortgage, lease,

sell, or purchase a plot of land for a period of up to 50 years (Ibrahim, 2018).

Ownership depends on the inhabitant of the investor/buyer, locals and foreigners

commonly possess different rights. Freehold ownership is applicable to UAE and Gulf

nationals (Bahraini, Kuwaiti, Omani, and Saudian) whose rights are equal to own and

invest in any area of Dubai, otherwise, non-gulf nationals are permitted for freehold

ownership or usufruct rights within the specified areas declared by Dubai's ruler

(Jadalhaq, 2017). Dubai has 23 special areas where foreigners can either acquire a

freehold ownership or usufruct while the area in plot no 224 of the Nad Al Sheba,

restricts the foreigners to obtain usufruct ownership or long period lease (Ibrahim, 2018).

Abu Dhabi, Dubai, Sharjah, and Umm Al Quwain laws follow the same rules for

real estate ownership. Ajman local laws complement to local laws in Dubai in terms of

equality, the right to ownership of land or real estate among the UAE and GCC nationals,

perhaps, the Ajman's ruler granted an unlimited freehold ownership or usufruct of any land for a period of 50 years for non-GCC foreigners (Jadalhaq, 2017). In Fujairah and

Ras Al Khaimah's law, the ruler owns all the lands within the emirate and only has the

power to grant ownership exclusively for UAE nationals, thus, Ras Al Khaimah's ruler

may grant ownership through: (a) habitual, as well as agriculture grant, restricted for

UAE nationals, except if the ruler designated an individual; and (b) investment and

charity grants are still based on the approval of the ruler (Ibrahim, 2018).

The real estate industry in UAE contributes to achieving sustainable development.

As part of strategic management, federal legislators protected the property investments of

nationals and foreigners, through laws and regulations. Dubai Land Department (DLD)

execute the most valuable aspect in real estate activities, in which all the legal processing

occurs, starting from the real estate developers to brokers, property registration and

transfer, documenting property sale and purchase, and other related procedures to real

estate ownership (Al Faris & Soto, 2016). DLD comprises of (a) the Real Estate

Regulatory Agency, also known as RERA, the regulatory arm; (b) the Real Estate

Investment Management & Promotion Center, the investment arm; (c) the Rental Dispute

Settlement Center, the Judicial arm; and (d) the Dubai Real Estate Institute, the

educational arm. Legislators entrusted RERA the following tasks for the real estate

sector: (a) proposing real estate legislations, (b) issuing regulations as per the law, (c)

licensing all real estate development activities, (d) accrediting financial institutions

(escrow accounts), and (e) regulating and monitoring real estate brokerages. No real

estate brokers and developers may engage in any real estate activities without a license

from RERA (Jadalhaq, 2017).

Geopolitical anxiety, deficiency of oil, and global investment market sentiment causes capital fluctuations and migratory pressures in UAE's real estate market. Residential Valuation System (RVS) helped to modify issues through the factors affecting valuation, the institutional capacity, ontological complexity, market dynamics, and information asymmetry (Huston, Lahbash, & Parsa, 2015). The UAE's RVS may contribute to sustainable residential market, institutional capabilities, standards salience, and trust. Conversely, Hafeez et al. (2016) studied the effective role of place branding and image to Dubai's traditional clusters such as the trading, tourism, and logistics, in which the continuous success affects the new clusters including the financial sector, construction, and real estate. Place branding aims to establish a positive image or a certain strategic marketing to develop the place competitiveness wherein the value of stakeholders (foreign investors, local businesses, citizens, and tourists) and the clusters (supporting firms or industries) are necessity; thus, some cities utilized semi-autonomous organizations to improve regional identity and overall image through marketing and branding despite high investment (Hafeez et al., 2016).

Nationality is one of the various factors that may influence property investors. Bajpai and Bhalchandra (2015) examined the rational and irrational factors that influence the investors/buyers in purchasing real estate property in Dubai amongst UAE, European/US Arab, and Asia nationals. Rational factors are physical structure, location, finance, and environmental whereas irrational involves psychological, emotional, intuitional, socialization (Anastasia & Suwitro, 2015). The researchers indicated that UAE and European/US nationals prioritize emotional and socialization factors upon investing a property, while Asian nationals and even Arab, prefers financial aspect (Bajpai & Bhalchandra, 2015).

Competitive Advantage

Competitive advantage is wide and complex, and one must identify the difference of concept and the sources. Sigalas (2015) defined the concept of competitive advantage pertains to the performance that involves high relative profitability, above average returns, benefit-cost gap, superior financial performance, economic profits, positive differential profits in excess of opportunity costs, and cross-sectional differential in the spread between product market demand and marginal cost. While the sources of competitive advantage include the properties of individual product markets, cost leadership, differentiation, locations, technologies, product features and firm's resources and capabilities (Sigalas, 2015). Bustinza, Bigdelim, Baines and Elliot (2015) emphasized that increasing differentiation and high customer satisfaction are fundamental to achieve competitive advantage and superior performance with services. Thus, the research indicated the importance of a company's position in the value chain and the organizational structure. Tan and Sousa (2015) also proved the role of low-cost and differentiation advantage in the relationship between marketing capabilities and export performance. Eloranta and Turunen (2015) analyzed the competitive advantage through the service infusion and strategy literature composes of four strategic management theories, the competitive forces, the resource-based view, dynamic capabilities, and relational view.

In strategy literature, the innovation of competitive advantage continuously grows just as the competition in the market. Gabrielsson, Seppala, and Gabrielsson (2016) emphasized the importance of hybrid strategy than single strategy especially in the high technology market as part of the globalization phase. Salavou (2015) also added the single-emphasis towards a hybrid form of competitive advantage, the mixed-emphasis, no-distinctive-emphasis, and stuck-in-the-middle that concerns conceptualization, reflecting to reality and the relationship between competitive strategy and firm performance. For instance, Uber took these strategies into innovated hybrid competitive advantage from driving down costs and reconstructing boundaries to focusing on the needs of the customers and creating an increase in value for buyers (Hales & Mclarney, 2017).

Strategic Management

Strategic management is one of the keys to attain and sustain competitive advantage in various industries. Dyer et al. (2016) studied the flow of strategic management process to achieve competitive advantage begins with the company's mission then identifying the strengths, weaknesses, opportunities, and threats factors proceeding on the formulation of the strategy followed by implementation. Giurgiu and Borza (2015) added the involvement of internal stakeholders or the human resources and shareholders and external stakeholders or the clients, suppliers, competitors, the environment, and society in implementing futuristic strategies to develop a competitive advantage.

Strategic management involves all levels and aspects of a business. Svarova and Vrchota (2014) explored the significance of strategic management towards competitive advantage which includes corporate level strategy formulated by the top management, developed by the middle-level management and applied by the lower level management. The management modifies the competitive advantage based on the labor quality, sentiment, flexibility, know-how, personal approach, and goodwill. Lev (2017) emphasized the value of corporate capabilities and assets like value-creating assets in creating and sustaining competitive advantage. However, the strategies commonly prioritize the quality, customer's satisfaction, stabilization on the market, innovation, expenditure, and revenue rise (Svarova & Vrchota, 2014). Su, Linderman, Schroeder, and Van de Ven (2014) researched the concept of sustaining both the high level and high consistency of quality performance with three capabilities including meta-learning, sensing weak signals, and resilience to quality disruptions.

Business owners create strategies but may fail to implement these strategies, causing a lack of competitive advantage. According to Harrigan (2017), strategic flexibility serves as an organizational regulation towards the growing competitive conditions and certain restructurings. Managerial perspectives and practices learned to reposition the assets and capabilities for new strategic aspirations and conquering an inevitable environmental change (Harrigan, 2017). Mishra (2017) indicated a firm's competitive advantage is enhanced by entrepreneurial incentives which increase the learning, adaptation, agility, and cognition of the management logics. Management logics develop the value creation and appropriation mechanism of the firm and extends the advantage through the opportunities, resources, strategic positions, events and challenges (Mishra, 2017). Chartres (2014) studied the relationship between the competitive advantage (efficiency of a franchise, ownership direction, and importance of the brand) and operational advantage (technology and internet) in the Australian real estate industry as a competitive advantage for an organization to survive and grow. Chartres (2014) broadened the franchising innovative strategies to achieve a success such as the correct implementation of business systems, training systems, recruitment of good operators.

In the real estate industry, there are various competitive advantage strategies that might contribute possible strategies depending on the market, location and the industry itself. Oladokun and Aluko (2015) concluded that corporate real estate management strategies used by over 69% of companies in Nigeria for productivity and competitive advantage either with private companies, public organizations or government department. While the rest had no corporate real estate management strategy and have different approaches such as cost reduction, facilitate production, flexibility, promote human resource objectives, promote the marketing message, promote sales and selling delivery, facilitate managerial process and knowledge, and capture real estate value (Oladokun & Aluko, 2015). Cengel and Oztek (2014) examined the impact of customer relation management as a competitive marketing strategy in the Turkish real estate that played a vital role. The marketing strategy shall take into considerations of the competition, mortgage, real estate standards, the need of certification for real estate agent, foreign customers and investors entering the market, and the need for safe properties for natural calamities (Cengel & Oztek, 2014). Gupta (2017) researched the focus on marketing strategies considering the challenges of the real estate industry in a Bangladesh-based company including a high rate of urbanization, densely populated urban areas with high demand for residential projects, and economic and life cycle of the sector.

Business leaders may create ideas and turn them into plans by identifying the factors affecting the business. Reshidi, Hoxha, and Zuferi (2015) examined the importance of the internal and external factors through the development of the real estate industry, greatly influenced by the employees, customers, and suppliers. Construction companies are one of the main suppliers providing the demands of the real estate industry, where they explore the needs of the customer; however, they do not commit with marketing strategies but plans on the realization of sales accordingly (Reshidi et al., 2015). Hakkak and Ghodsi (2015) examined the relevance of balanced scorecard as a strategic tool to evaluate the financial and market position of a firm that measures the aspects of financial, customer, internal process, and growth and learning for a sustainable competitive advantage. The researchers stated that balanced scorecard creates a balance through long-term and short-term objectives, financial and non-financial measures, leader and follower indicators, internal and external performance (Hakkak & Ghodsi, 2015).

Strengths and Weaknesses

Customer, employees, resources, capabilities, and process (innovation). The common strengths and weaknesses of a business are the consumers, people, assets, skills, and the methods. Davis (2017) identified internal views for firm competitive advantage pertaining to increase employee heterogeneity and a decrease in resource mobility. The findings show how the human resources can use employees as the resource-based theory for firm's competitive advantage (Davis, 2017). Albrecht, Bakker, Gruman, Macey, and Saks (2015) researched the interrelationships between the organizational context factors and HRM practices such as personnel selection, socialization, performance management, and training and development influence organizational outcomes and competitive advantage. Sikora, Thompson, Russell, and Ferris (2016) also examined the effectiveness of human capital and resource-based theory into a long-term competitive advantage. The study indicated that hiring overqualified job candidates are beneficial, in contrast, organizations lower its cost amongst highly skilled human capital (Sikora et al., 2016). In relation to environmental changes and issues, Aykan (2017) researched the significance of green human resource management (GHRM) to environmental sustainability and gaining competitive advantage. The researcher indicated the GHRM functions and practices include green job analysis and design, green human resources planning, green recruitment, green selection, green induction, green performance assessment, green training and development, green rewarding system, green job safety, green discipline management, and green employee relations (Aykan, 2017).

People play a vital role in a business or organization, starting from the highest to lowest position, from the activities to practices. Delery and Roumpi (2017) discussed the tension between the strategic human resource management (SHRM) and strategic human capital among its different approach over the resource-based view of a firm. Delery and Roumpi (2017) argued the human resource management (HRM) practices and activities as human capital resources that contribute to a firm's sustainable competitive advantage through ability-motivation-opportunity (AMO) model towards employees along with shaping supply and demand side mobility constraints. HRM activities are investment and intensive training, selective staffing, performance appraisals, team building, and firm-specific skills (knowledge, skills, and abilities) while HRM practices being associated with human capital, consist of tools including firm specify, social complexity, and causal ambiguity (Delery & Roumpi, 2017). However, Coff and Raffiee (2015) agreed that firm-specific human capital is a source of sustained competitive advantage but limits employee mobility or flexibility. Firm-specific skills are valuable within a focal firm compare to general skills that are easily transferable that makes it harder to apply and may experience decreased productivity, thus, micro literature rarely acknowledges the firm-specific human capital for being crucial to value creation and appropriation (Coff & Raffiee, 2015). Prajogo and Oke (2016) confirmed the positive effect of human capital towards competitive advantage and business performance influenced by the service innovation advantage (new service features, new processes, new technologies, and new methods). Resource-based theory composes of resources, capabilities, and assets that are rare, valuable, non-substitutable, and difficult to imitate which includes human capital as an intangible resource or intellectual capital utilizing individual's creativity, knowledge, and skills (Prajogo & Oke, 2016).

The kind of leadership that leaders impose on followers may reflect on the actions either positively or negatively. According to Mittal and Dhar (2015), creative self-efficacy (CSE) mediates the relationship between the transformational leadership and employee creativity, which serves as one of the approaches to attaining and sustaining competitive advantage. The study presented that through transformational leadership style, a leader may establish CSE and employee creativity to enhance the skills and

acquire knowledge for higher performance (Mittal & Dhar, 2015). Conversely, Higgs and

Dulewicz (2016) studied the impact of leadership thinking or how the leaders require

emotional intelligence to lead effectively for competitive advantage strategies.

Building a rapport between the customers and employees develops the

relationship of the business towards the market. Kumar and Pansari (2016) added the

need for engagement as the framework to a sustainable competitive advantage that

involves the customer engagement and employee engagement, both positively influence a

firm performance, although the customer engagement is stronger. Krajnakova, Navikaite,

and Navickas (2015) examined the management of customer satisfaction as the key for

competitive advantage particularly in small and medium-sized enterprises that consists of

repeat buying, higher prices, word of mouth, new product innovation, loyalty in crises,

and one-stop shopping. Krajnakova et al. (2015) added the possible long-term strategies

involving the customer relationship management to sustain competitive advantage which

involves the customer's loyalty, trust, retention, and satisfaction. Jensen (2015) agreed on

creating and maintaining relationships with the consumers in the markets for a

sustainable competitive advantage. The researcher indicated the customer value for

marketing strategy in satisfying the consumers with knowledge, experience and

expectations (Jensen, 2015). Caldwell, Licona, and Floyd (2015) explored the ability of

internal marketing through strong customer relationships and highly committed

employees that allows the organizations to attain competitive advantage. The researchers

identified propositions to create effective strategies which involve wealth creation (leadership and employee behavior), ethical decision-making, high-performance management system, understanding organizational citizen, and invest in creating a learning culture (Caldwell et al., 2015).

Apart from the customers and employees, the next important factor to consider in creating such strategies are the resources of the business. Liu and Liang (2015) explored the resource-based operations strategy supported with sense and respond approach for decision-making to sustainable competitive advantage in a high-tech manufacturing industry with resource allocation as the key to an operational competitiveness performance. Huang, Dyerson, Wu, and Harindranath (2015) explained that firms with a stronger market position can only attain a temporary competitive advantage while firms that possess a superior position in technological resources or capabilities attain a sustainable competitive advantage. Thus, industrial organization (IO) and the resource−based view (RBV) verified the outcome variables of competitive advantage (Huang et al., 2015). Balashova and Gromova (2016) analyzed the implementation of the principles of resource-based view or the modern resource management in providing firm's long-term competitive advantage. Balashova and Gromova (2016) discussed the method of dynamic capabilities in implementing the resource-based view which is a part of organizational capabilities (core competencies and operating/functional capabilities) wherein the capacity of the company integrates, build and reconfigure internal and external competencies in adjustment to the growth of the environment.

Adapting and adjusting to constant changes in the competitive market requires newer sources. Alonso-Almeida, Bremser, and Llach (2015) explored the influence of dynamic capabilities to improve competitive advantage along with proactive strategies during a financial crisis. The researchers indicated the objective of the proactive strategy includes market leadership (prospector), operational efficiency (defender), or both (analyzer); thus, dynamic capabilities create and modify its resource base such as reconfiguring, a process of discontinuing certain practices or eliminating unnecessary routines (Alonso-Almeida et al., 2015). Bellner and MacLean (2015) researched the significance of dynamic managerial capabilities (DMC) in attaining and sustaining competitive advantage through strategic management. Learning-based (acquisition of knowledge), innovation-based (introducing new ideas, methods, products, and services), participative leadership (engagement of employee), and relational capacities (firm's allies) are the core of dynamic capabilities used by the managers during external environmental change (Bellner & MacLean, 2015). Sugiono, Arifianti, Raharja, Maulina, and Hapsari (2017) suggested there is a relationship between dynamic capabilities and organizational knowledge in building competitive advantage. Sugiono et al. (2017) stated the essential components to the competitiveness of an organization are the resource-based and knowledge capabilities.

Dynamic capability is an approach to understand the newer sources of competitive advantage. Felin and Powell (2016) described dynamic capability as a theory of competitive advantage, organizations create the capacity to sense, shape, and seize new market opportunities for strategy, innovation, and designing organizations. Wamba et al. (2017) confirmed the role of process-oriented dynamic capabilities such as coordination, integration, cost reduction, and business intelligence on the relationship between firm performance and big data analytics as a new enabler of competitive advantage. Wamba et al. (2017) defined big data analytics as the ability to support business insights utilizing data management, infrastructure, and talent competence to establish the business into a competitive force. Furthermore, Ransbotham, Kiron, and Prentice (2015) examined analytics as a competitive advantage through consumption of data and analytics as well as not just in production but with business issues. Ransbotham et al. (2015) indicated analytics sophistication towards consumption and production increases and produce complexity. Managers perform analytical skills to inflate consuming analytics through bolstering the knowledge base, building off prior experience, creating analytical options, capitalizing on domain knowledge, and recognizing the limitations of models (Ransbotham et al., 2015).

Technology is one of the biggest contributors of innovative strategies. Ashrafi and Mueller (2015) evaluated the value of information technology (IT) capabilities that generates more business effects in dynamics environments, creates competitive advantage and boost the financial performance of a firm rather than IT resources (Human, Knowledge, and Relationship resources) that works in a stable environment. Furthermore, IT investments also symbolizes an alignment between the IT resources and business strategies including the organizational ability of internal business processes to adjust with rapid changes (Mao et al., 2016).

Innovation

Innovation may have a positive impact on a company's ability to attain and sustain competitive advantage. Brem, Maier, and Wimschneider (2016) indicated the success of a company through the application of strategy with proper alignment to develop a unique market position. Innovation includes the product itself, affiliating with other businesses, and selecting a diverse distribution channel such as online, phone calls or exclusive boutiques (Brem et al., 2016). Aziz and Samad (2016) also agreed how innovation build up competitive advantage through the firm's assets, capabilities, characteristics, information and knowledge.

Innovation management could create an advantage over competitors locally and internationally. Dereli (2015) determined the factors of innovation as the key to success includes organizational structure and culture, technology, human factor, team management, productivity, and research and development; hence, an innovative approach varies in lifestyle and environment, customer-oriented way, time and application, effectivity, competition, failures, investigation, atmosphere, and technology. Taneja, Pryor, and Hayek (2016) studied innovation as one of the key drivers of sustainable competitive advantage. Small businesses contribute to the economic growth of many nations which also creates opportunities, employment, and technological development. Thus, business leaders integrate innovation to remain competitive and achieve long-term sustainability and viability. Strategic innovation elements compose of: (a) passion for creating, inventing, and innovating; (b) cooperation, collaboration and co-opetition; (c) resources, skills, and management capabilities; (d) organizational culture, structure, and streamlined processes; and (e) supportive customers, suppliers, and employees (Taneja et al., 2016).

Innovation may compose of internal and external resources including technical and technological aspects. Noorani (2014) investigated the concept of service innovation in attaining competitive advantage using the resource-based view including the human resources (customer relations), information technology (innovation), and research and development (channel of distribution). The researcher identified human resources as responsible for the service quality, while research and development accountable with organizational knowledge and target market, and the information technology liable for internal and external competitive sources (Noorani, 2014). According to Sitek (2017), innovation stimulates competitiveness in the real estate market. The group of innovations in the real estate industry involves technical and technological (modern solutions from designing stage to implementation to measuring and operation), process and organizational (technical innovations, legal changes, and adjustments to requirements), marketing (sales and distribution of products and services), and financial (investment activities such as derivatives, mortgage bonds, reverse mortgage, green mortgage, and bancassurance) (Sitek, 2017).

Innovation connects to many aspects of the business. Liao, Rice, and Lu (2015) studied that in creating or sustaining competitive advantage, the interaction is a necessity between firm's innovation investments, effective market engagement activities, and operations for innovation to sustain or improve financial performance. The researchers indicated environmental fitness or market transformation as the mediator between innovation activities and firm performance, as well as the influence of dynamic capabilities in creating, extending or modifying the resources of a firm towards innovation and market transformation (Research and development, training, marketing and production system improvement); hence, market transformation is the primary and direct driver of firm performance (Liao et al., 2015). While Belenzon and Tsolmon (2015) examined the competitive advantage of internal labor markets, especially in manufacturing small and medium enterprises. The researchers studied the ability of internal labor market through redeploying of workers with restrictions and imposing strict employment protection laws. However, labor flexibility might also be a stronger source of competitive advantage in countries with developed financial markets that offer more flexible capital adjustments or so-called market frictions (Belenzon & Tsolmon, 2015).

Marketing takes the responsibilities in promoting the results of innovation towards products and services. Aghazadeh (2015) investigated the role of intelligent marketing strategy (IMS) in sustaining competitive advantage and achieve superior performance. The study specified the internal capabilities and external position in creating a sustainable competitive advantage, applying innovative knowledge, developing marketing information and relationship in building value creation, attraction, and satisfaction towards customer, market, and financial performance (Aghazadeh, 2015). Ladipo, Awoniyi, and Arebi (2017) added the components of marketing intelligence that consists of internal record, competitor's sales data, marketplace opportunity, competitors' threat, and competitive risk, and its relationship between business competitive advantage like profitability, sales turnover, market share, productivity, and effectiveness.

Business leaders also focus on the marketing process to create an effective and efficient strategy. Jahanshahi, Nawaser, Eizi, and Etemadi (2015) studied the role of real options reasoning to increase market orientation and organizational learning in attaining and sustaining competitive advantage. Market orientation enriches profitability, performance, and increase employee's commitment to the organization while organizational learning is an antecedent or consequence of market orientation but interact positively with each other (Jahanshahi et al., 2015). Real options thinking is a low-risk strategy particularly in SMEs through its capability of resource allocation processes in terms of market, technology, and a dynamic business environment (Jahanshahi et al., 2015). Conversely, Coccia (2016) researched a case in medicine industry that problem-driven innovation through radical and incremental supports the competitive advantage of firms characterized by competitive intensity, and technological and market dynamism.

Dynamic capabilities and innovation may increase firm performance with the support of organizational learning. Kalmuk and Acar (2015) examined the effectivity of organizational learning capability towards innovation (technological and administrative) and firm's performance to gain a sustainable competitive advantage. The researchers identified organizational and administrative characteristics (organizational learning capability) as the element to develop the firm's capabilities comprising of four sub-processes; obtaining information, distribution of information, interpretation of information and stored the accumulated information for future purposes (Kalmuk & Acar, 2015). Giniuniene and Jurksiene (2015) added that organizational learning is an important part of dynamic capabilities, a primary source of competitive advantage. Hence, organizational learning processes also mediate innovation and dynamic capabilities to increase firm performance (Giniuniene & Jurksiene, 2015). However,

Butnariu and Avasilcai (2015) studied the influence of innovation on environmental management and competitive advantage based on costs and differentiation. The researchers indicated continuous innovation to processes, products, and systems are the most influential factor compare to the other resource-based of a firm such as the capabilities of integrate stakeholders and organizational learning (Butnariu & Avasilcai, 2015).

Innovation process includes the ability to identify and absorb new knowledge. Lis and Sudolska (2015) added the relationship between the absorptive capacity and open innovation in creating competitive advantage. The absorptive capacity process includes knowledge recognition, acquisition, assimilation, transformation, and exploitation performed and engaged by the executives and employees along with the combination of open innovation using its own knowledge resources improves the performance and growth of the firm (Lis & Sudolska, 2015). Absorptive capacity originally came from the concept of the resource-based view, the knowledge-based view, and dynamic capability (Seo, Chae, & Lee, 2015). Chuang et al. (2016) investigated the influence of collective learning and absorptive capacity towards the relationship of social capital and competitive advantage, which requires a higher knowledge management to respond faster on competitive challenges of a firm. Social capital impacts competitive advantage through relationships and interactions of the firm to the society, as well as its resources and capabilities (Chuang et al., 2016). Furthermore, collective learning promotes an interactive process to accumulate knowledge from different learning resources, channels and opportunities while absorptive capacity refers to the ability of a firm to obtain, absorb, and convert the knowledge into dynamic organizational capabilities (Chuang et al., 2016). Conversely, Lau and Lo (2015) identified the absorptive capacity as the knowledge for developing operational capabilities in achieving competitive advantage with four distinctive processes: (a) identify and acquire external knowledge; (b) analyze, process, interpret, and understand the acquired knowledge; (c) build and purify existing and newly acquired knowledge; (d) exploit existing and transformed knowledge into operations. In order to enhance the absorptive capacity of the firm and innovation performance, the researchers use the regional innovation system (RIS) to adapt, generate, and extend knowledge from public and private agents with its elements: (a) regional innovation initiatives, private and government innovation activities of the region; (b) knowledge-intensive business services or services for economic activities; and (c) value chain information sources or gain information from suppliers, customers, and competitors (Lau & Lo, 2015).

Innovation requires intellectual capital in creating and developing a competitive advantage strategy. Chatzoglou and Chatzoudes (2018) indicated the positive direct and indirect effects of innovation on the creation of competitive advantages through knowledge management, intellectual capital, organizational capabilities and organizational culture. Ngah et al. (2015) studied the intellectual capital, knowledge management, and innovation intelligence as the key to exploring the opportunities using the resources and capabilities for a sustainable competitive advantage. Chahal and Bakshi (2015) studied the direct and positive impact of intellectual capital on the competitive advantage. The researcher confirmed how innovation played a role in creating intellectual capital and building a sustainable competitive advantage for organizations in the banking

sector along with the organizational learning (Chahal & Bakshi, 2015). In essence,

Todericiu and Stanit (2015) agreed to the efficiency of intellectual capital for a

sustainable competitive advantage and long-term development along with the intangible

resources. The researchers noted the human capital includes employee skills, expertise,

and know-how; relational capital such as customer, supplier, and other external

relationships; and structural capital or the intangible assets as the intellectual capital of a

firm (Todericiu & Stanit, 2015). Lee, Foo, Leong, and Ooi (2016) validated the positive

impact of knowledge management through managerial practices of knowledge sharing,

application, and storage towards technological innovation and competitive advantage.

Thus, technological innovation significantly affects competitive advantage and

technological innovation connects knowledge management and competitive advantage

(Lee et al., 2016).

Internal resources may consider as profits when use and control accordingly.

Ahmad (2015) investigated the concept of business intelligence (BI) in strategic

management as an essential tool for competitive advantage. The findings showed the

internal resources for organizations including the BI governance with strong moral and

financial support, while the perceptions of BI's characteristics involve complexity,

compatibility, and observability that influence a successful implementation of business

intelligence (Ahmad, 2015). Amiri, Shirkavand, Chalak, and Rezaeei (2017) examined

the competitive intelligence as a means of a competitive advantage with insurance companies using the knowledge from internal and external environments for planning, collecting, analyzing, sharing and evaluating information.

Opportunities and Threats: Social, Environmental, and Financial Factors

The factors affecting opportunities and threats are social, environmental, and financial aspects. Schulz and Flanigan (2016) used the Triple Bottom Line or considering the social, environmental, and financial factors as a tool for competitive advantage. The findings developed a model involving environmental and social responsibility scales with a combination of financial data (Schulz & Flanigan, 2016). Kwarteng, Dadzie, and Famiyeh (2016) elaborated the approach of triple bottom line along with corporate social responsibility and stakeholder theory to which firms sustain competitive advantage. The study indicated the positive impact of economic and social factors to corporate image, in which corporate image and social factors create a positive corporate performance, on the contrary, economic and environment may not have a direct impact toward a corporate performance (Kwarteng et al., 2016). De Guimarães, Andréa Severo, and de Vasconcelos (2017) explored the relationship between organizational performance and sustainable competitive advantage along with the attributes of environmental sustainability and social responsibility.

Environmental factors could establish valuable impact in attaining competitive advantage. According to Molina-Azorín et al. (2015), environmental management improves competitive advantage through costs and differentiation and enhances the relationship with stakeholders. Firms adopting proactive environmental strategies save costs, inputs and energy, and re-use materials which reduces the use of resources (cost) and pollution (differentiation) may gain consumers whose particular with environmental features (Molina-Azorín et al., 2015). Virapongse et al. (2016) used social-ecological system (SES) approach in facing environmental changes that are commonly caused by addressing broader scales, conflicting stakeholder worldviews, managing for abrupt change and adaptability, scale mismatch, institutional limitations, and lack of empirical evidence. Thus, SES helps address the current challenges through systemic worldview, transdisciplinary approaches, adaptive governance, monitoring systems, and education and training (Virapongse et al., 2016). Colvin, Witt, and Lacey (2015) extended the environmental management literature by the essential component, the stakeholder engagement. Hence, engaging stakeholders in decision-making not only promote sustainable development but understanding the issues of environmental and natural resources (Colvin et al., 2015).

Environmental and social factors are part of changing demands on the competitive market. Yadav, Han, and Kim (2016) investigated the effect of environmental performance as part of a corporate strategy in developing unique environmental resources along with an economic value sustains competitive advantage. In essence, Dangelico and Pontrandolfo (2015) discovered the difference between environmental management and firm performance as a competitive advantage, which varies on the type of environmental focus (materials, energy, pollution) and collaborations with business and non–business actors. Vanpoucke, Vereecke, and Wetzels (2014) studied the ability to adapt to changing environments in creating a sustainable competitive advantage through supplier integrative capability by integration sensing, seizing opportunities and transforming changes. Roy and Karna (2015) researched the capabilities of social entrepreneurship (SE) to achieve a competitive advantage with an alliance to a resource-based view which involves the reputation and network of the founder, managerial knowledge and experience, and other corporate resources of the business. The researchers added the frequent basis of competitive advantage begins with the management that is strengthened through the support of the institutional environment (Roy & Karna, 2015). According to Gregory, Whittaker, and Yan (2016) associated corporate social performance (CSP) with the competitive advantage that generates higher coefficient on earnings and increases firm value.

Corporate social responsibility may commonly associate with social factors. Moczadlo (2015) examined the corporate social responsibility as a long-term business strategy considering the economic, social, and environmental matter with ethical human rights and consumer concerns as a core element for competitive advantage. CSR started as a social movement for civil rights, women's rights, consumers, and environmentalism, then evolved into corporate social responsiveness to corporate social performance that involves business ethics, corporate citizenship, sustainability, and stakeholder management (Carroll, 2015). According to Ağan, Kuzey, Acar, and Açıkgöz (2016), sustainability consists of four aspects: (a) strategy, the activities to surpass sustainability issues; (b) risk management, planning the possibilities of upstream and downstream; (c) organizational culture, the ethical standards; and (d) transparency, the traceability and controllability. Saedi et al. (2015) explained that CSR and firm performance has no direct relationship but rather a mediated relationship through reputation and competitive advantage while improving the level of customer satisfaction on Iranian manufacturing and consumer product firms. CSR composes of economic, legal, ethical, and discretionary, hence, CSR operations have a positive association with the determinants of a firm's performance including monetary performance, personal commitment, and corporate integrity (Saedi et al., 2015). However, researchers argued the components for sustainable competitive advantage are the customer satisfaction and reputation, an outcome of firm performance and customer satisfaction which results in loyalty and productivity for meeting the customer's expectations over the product or service.

Social and environmental factors may influence one another. Wang, Dou, and Jia (2015) discussed the relationship between CSR and corporate financial performance (CFP), and the moderators, the measurement strategy, and environmental context. In previous studies, the five kinds of measurement strategies consist of CSR reputation ratings, content analysis, surveys, social auditing database, and proxy variable (Wang et al., 2015). Ağan et al. (2016) indicated the influence of corporate social responsibility (CSR) towards environmental supplier development (ESD) which results positively to financial performance and competitive advantage of the firms, particularly in manufacturing firms. CSR is based on ethical values that involves the employees, customers, environment, media, and partnerships with non-government organizations while ESD is a cooperative effort of the buying firms and suppliers to reduce environmental impact and increase capabilities, thus, CSR influences ESD in helping the suppliers to develop environmentally safe products, processes, and technology through evaluative and collaborative activities or apply supplier evaluation, incentives, and direct involvement (Ağan et al., 2016).

Researchers have studied the potential of HR practices as a source of competitive advantage through human capital utilizing the resource-based approach. Jiang and Liu (2015) extended the human resources management literature to the contextual complement of human capital, the social capital which mediates the relationship between high-performance work system (HPWS) and organizational performance. HPWS influences intra-organizational social capital in terms of staffing, self-managed teams, and flexible job assignment, self-managed teams and compensation, training, open communication, staffing, and decentralized decision-making. Thus, social capital factors impact on organizational effectiveness through favorable interpersonal environment, organizational innovation, and knowledge transfer (Jiang & Liu, 2015). Whipple, Wiedmer, and Boyer (2015) also added the role of social capital between collaborative process competence and operational performance, in which both internal and external collaborative relationships can improve a firm's competitive advantage. The social capital consists of three aspects: (a) structural, the linkages of people or pattern of connections, (b) relational, the assets gained and embedded, and (c) cognitive, the shared vision), hence, these dimensions improve a buyer-supplier relationship and develop firm performance (Whipple, Wiedmer, & Boyer, 2015).

Transition

In Section 1, I provided an overview of competitive advantage strategies during a global financial crisis or unstable market, particularly in the real estate industry. Real estate companies are overwhelmed because of the growing competition from different industry and within the sector. Thus, businesses experience poor performance and profitability which led to survive but not to earn. I also discussed different strategies from different industries that might benefit real estate business leaders. Hence, I conducted a multiple case study of four real estate business leaders in Dubai, UAE to explore strategies to attain and sustain competitive advantage to increase profitability during periods of unstable or declining markets. In Section 2, I present the research procedure with a detailed explanation of the role of the researcher, the participants, the research method and design, population and sampling, ethical research, data collection instruments and techniques, data organization techniques, data analysis, reliability and validity, transition and summary. In Section 3, I present the findings, application to professional practice, implications for social change, recommendations for action and further research, reflections, and conclusions.

Section 2: The Project

In this study, I focused on competitive advantage strategies that real estate business leaders use to increase profitability during periods of unstable or declining markets. The strengths, weaknesses, opportunities, and threats of a business are the factors required to identify competitive advantage strategies (Dyer et al., 2016). In this section, I describe how I gained access to my target participants, the real estate business leaders. I was the main instrument to collect data for this study of participants' competitive advantage strategies. The major topics I discuss in Section 2 include the role of the researcher, the research method, research design, the participants, and ethical consideration in research.

Purpose Statement

The purpose of this qualitative multiple case study was to explore the strategies Dubai real estate business leaders use to attain and sustain competitive advantage to increase profitability during periods of unstable or declining markets. The study population consisted of four real estate business leaders in the regions of Dubai, an emirate that has demonstrated success within the UAE and the Middle East. Interviewees were active and licensed brokers, participating in both off plan and ready units, handling both residential and commercial properties, and working within both sales and lease markets. The implications for positive social change include the potential to establish economic growth within the industry, potentially, adding value to larger communities by stabilizing markets, strengthening the local economy, and potentially improving families' lifestyles. In addition, investors or expatriates may make investments in the real estate sector that could promote the unique culture and society of UAE.

Role of the Researcher

As the researcher, my role included accumulating and exploring data gathered from the research participants. According to Fusch and Ness (2015), the researcher is an instrument for data collection which makes the researcher inseparable from the research. However, the researcher carries the responsibility of comprehending one own's perspectives regarding a participant's cultural world. The researcher's cultural and experiential background creates biases, value, and ideologies; thus, data triangulation might help novice researchers through multiple data sources to mitigate bias (Fusch, Fusch, & Ness, 2017; Joslin & Muller, 2016).

I operate and work for a real estate business in Kuwait. However, I do not have any business relationship with the real estate agencies in Dubai, or with the research participants. To separate my own perspectives and the participants' cultural worlds, I expressed my personal thoughts or statements about the research through field notes or journals to write everything I saw and heard. Moreover, the notes served as a tool for reflections to understand and ensure that my interpretations accurately represented participants' views and not my personal lens (Maharaj, 2016). Journals and field notes also help researchers identify key themes and patterns in the data that can also enhance the validity of the research (Fusch, Fusch, & Ness, 2017; Greenwood et al., 2017).

To outline ethical principles for conducting research involving humans as subjects, the United States integrated the Belmont Report into regulations and law

(Grady, 2015). The Belmont Report serves as an ethical guideline for the protection of human subjects of research (Friesen, Kearns, Redman, & Caplan, 2016). The Belmont report has three core principles: (a) respect for persons, the guiding principle, holds that people are autonomous and have the right to make their own choices and decisions, whether they like to participate or not and the like; (b) beneficence, the principle of doing good and creating no harm, increase potential benefits and decrease possible adverse events; and (c) justice, a central principle, requires equal treatment and fairness for all people (Miracle, 2016).

To address the possibility of personal bias, I used data collection methods such as interview protocol, semistructured interviews, field notes, participant observation, and member checking. Because the case study design delimits the study in time and space (Fusch, Fusch, & Ness, 2017), the multiple sources of data mitigated personal bias during the data collection process (Roulston & Shelton, 2015). A researcher is a data collection instrument itself which could create biases intentionally or unintentionally (Fusch & Ness, 2015). Hearing and understanding the perspective of the participants is one of the dilemmas of researchers, thus, it requires time to reflect and interpret the behavior of others.

Researchers use an interview protocol to ensure alignment between the interview and research questions, develop an inquiry-based conversation and receive feedback. Qualitative researchers can increase the quality of data acquired from research interviews by enhancing and refining the reliability of interview protocols (Castillo-Montoya, 2016). I used an interview protocol to ensure that my experiences did not influence data interpretation. The interview protocol contained demographic and research questions, supported with audio recordings and written notes. The protocol also included a follow-up interview and member checking with the participants to either confirm or add from the data collected. The use of multiple data sources and evidence might eliminate bias and ensure validity (Fusch & Ness, 2015; Roulston & Shelton, 2015).

Participants

The participants were real estate business leaders who had successfully attained and sustained competitive advantage to increase profitability during periods of unstable or declining markets. The study criteria required that participants be active and licensed brokers, participating in both off-plan and ready units, handling both residential and commercial properties, and working within both sales and lease markets. Participant selection includes having a clear rationale, purpose, and conceptual framework; hence, the participants could more likely produce rich and dense information in relation to the study's the research questions (Cleary, Horsfall, & Hayter, 2014; Gentles et al., 2015; Yin, 2017).

I used a combination of traditional and internet-mediated strategies to gain access to participants. I connected with the participants through email, text message and telephone conversation. I familiarized myself to the potential participant, made enough time, stated the purpose, addressed potential organizational concerns, identified possible benefits, utilized suitable language, was responsive, applied incremental strategy, and established credibility. Gaining access to organizations or individuals is one of the major tasks in collecting data and is a pre-requisite for conducting research (Peticca-Harris, DeGama, & Elias, 2016; Yin, 2014).

I used give-and-take interaction to establish a working relationship with the participants. I built a rapport before proceeding to the study. Trust is a key aspect of justice, one of the Belmont principles (Judkins-Cohn et al., 2014), while ethics involves the researcher's responsibilities towards the participants' dignity, privacy, and well-being (Wang & Geale, 2015). Relationships are built with attentiveness to the personalities, desires, needs, knowledge, and attentiveness to participants as human beings (Stahl, 2016). Furthermore, researchers must maintain boundaries to protect the researcher-participant relationship and ethical obligations to do no harm (Rossetto, 2014).

Research Method and Design

Research Method

Saunders et al. (2015) classified research methodology into three types: qualitative, quantitative, and mixed methods. Qualitative research is understanding the aspect of social life through the experience and attitudes of the subject; it answers questions to 'what', 'how', or 'why' of a phenomenon; ensures the quality of the process; involves the personality of the researcher; and establish the credibility and trustworthiness of the research findings (McCusker & Gunaydin, 2015; Noble & Smith, 2015). I determined that qualitative research was the most appropriate methodology for this study because of the explorative nature of the research question (Marshall & Rossman, 2016).

Quantitative research involves statistical data in the form of numbers and statistics, which answer *'how many'* or *'how much'* (McCusker & Gunaydin, 2015; Saunders et al., 2015). A quantitative method was not appropriate for this study because the study did not demand statistical data or numerical objectivity. Mixed methods research is a combination of a qualitative and quantitative method for collecting, analyzing, and interpreting data (Makrakis & Kostoulas-Makrakis, 2016). Neither the quantitative or mixed method would have been appropriate for the study; therefore, I selected the qualitative method.

Research Design

Research design is the general plan of how the researcher get answers from the research question, it contains clear objectives derived from the research question, indicates the sources from which and how to collect the data (Saunders et al., 2015). A qualitative case study was the most appropriate research design because the purpose of the study was to distinguish and explore the strategies real estate business leaders used to attain and sustain competitive advantage to increase profitability during periods of unstable or declining markets. The case study may address the interrelationship between the phenomenon and the context with the help of *'how'* or *'why'* questions of the phenomena (Yazan, 2015). A case study could either be a single case or multiple case; a single case mainly focuses on one business only while a multiple case captures a rich description of the context (Vohra, 2014). Therefore, I selected a qualitative multiple case study for the research.

In a qualitative research design, the principal research strategies are narrative, ethnography, phenomenology, and case study (Saunders et al., 2015). Narrative research is suited to exploring life stories and deals with personal experiences not with organizations (Kim, 2016). Ethnographic research focuses on investigation of the network of social groupings, customs, beliefs, behaviors, and practices (Percy, Kostere, & Kostere, 2015). Phenomenological research investigates the lived experiences of a phenomena which may include attitudes, beliefs, opinions, feelings, and the like (Percy et al., 2015). Neither the narrative, ethnography, or phenomenology would have been appropriate for the study; therefore, I selected case study to explore strategies that real estate business leaders used to attain and sustain competitive advantage to increase profitability during periods of unstable or declining markets.

I ensured data saturation with a spiral approach where planning, acting, observing, and reflecting takes place during data analysis until no new substantive information is acquired. Saturation is the building of rich data with scope or comprehensiveness until replication of essential data are identified (Morse, 2015). In qualitative research, researchers use purposeful sampling to identify and select information-rich cases through individuals who are knowledgeable or well-experienced related to the phenomenon (Palinkas et al., 2015); hence, purposive sampling methods place a primary emphasis on saturation (Etikan, 2016).

Population and Sampling

The population for this qualitative multiple case study were four real estate business leaders in Dubai, UAE that successfully attained and sustained competitive advantage to increase profitability during periods of unstable or declining markets. The main economic sources of UAE are oil and gas; however, the result of the global financial crisis urged the country to diversify into other sectors to reduce the dependence on the oil-based industry, in which the real estate market became one of the major industries (Bodolica, Spraggon, & Shahid, 2018; Sundarakani, 2017). In this study, I used a purposeful sampling method and selected four real estate business leaders who successfully attained and sustained competitive advantage. According to Gentles et al. (2015), saturation is the common criterion on distinguishing when sufficient sample size has been reached in a qualitative research, hence, bigger is not better but neither is smaller of a sample (Roy et al., 2015).

I used purposeful sampling in selecting the participants. Purposeful sampling applies specifically in a qualitative research to classify and select the information-rich cases relevant to the phenomenon (Palinkas et al., 2015). The four-point approach to sampling includes (a) defining the sample universe, (b) deciding the sample size, (c) devising the sampling strategy, and (d) sourcing the sample (Robinson, 2014). Patton (2015) stated that the logic and power of purposeful sampling lie in selecting information-rich cases for in-depth study, in which one can learn a great deal about issues of central importance to the purpose of the inquiry, and yields insights and in-depth understanding.

The participants were capable of providing rich answers to the research questions as they had a previous successful experience pertaining to the phenomenon. In purposive sampling, a researcher sets criteria for selecting the sample such as why recruit the individuals and what qualifies them (Haegele & Hodge, 2015; Palinkas et al., 2015). The setting for the interviews was in a meeting or conference room of a hotel in Downtown, Dubai, to have a good quality of recordings and where the participants was not get easily distracted. However, the participants are allowed to choose the settings for the interviews as long as they are comfortable and in a quiet environment (Dikko, 2016). Upon receiving the IRB approval and before the interviews, I confirmed and verified that the participants met the required qualifications and that all participants were eligible to participate in the research study.

Ethical Research

Ethical research may depend on the knowledge and integrity of the researcher; thus, everyone conducts research assumes a moral responsibility to abide by commonly accepted ethical standards (Workman, Kielhofner, & Taylor, 2017). The informed consent is an authorization or agreement that the participant/s understands the research and its risk, it is not merely a form that is signed but a process (Grady, 2015); therefore, I stated this information in the informed consent form which also contained my contact information, being the researcher, and Walden University's contact email and phone numbers as the IRB's responsible for approving the research involving human subjects to ensure compliance with the guidelines set for ethical research. The IRB procedures specify that research participation is voluntary (Connelly, 2014); hence, I explained that participation was voluntary and that participants may withdraw at any time before or during the interview. The participants received no compensation in exchange for their participation, however, each participant will receive a final approved copy of the study.

The Walden University institutional review board (IRB) approval number for this study is 01-17-19-0736211.

The ethical protection of a researcher involves the privacy and confidentiality of information and ensure minimal risks of the participants (Rashid, Caine, & Goez, 2015), wherefore I completed the training for Protecting Human Subject Research Participants by the National Institute of Health Training on Human Participants. I also used acronyms to protect the personal identities of the participants through the term P along with numbers in accordance to the order of the interview: P1, the first participant; P2, the second participant; P3, the third participant; and P4, the fourth participant. To protect the confidentiality of the participants, I will store the data securely for 5 years and destroy eventually as per the policy of Walden University.

Data Collection Instruments

I collected the data from the real estate agencies operating in Dubai and used semistructured interviews to explore the strategies to attain and sustain competitive advantage to increase profitability during periods of unstable or declining markets. Semistructured interviews provide the means of developing information-rich data sets in a time and resource efficient manner (O'Keeffe et al., 2016), hence, semistructured method enables reciprocity between the interviewer and participant (Kallio et al., 2016). For further analysis of the data, I utilized archival and document secondary data specifically the text materials including the organizations' databases, email and letters, social media and websites, articles and journals. Secondary data may provide the main source to answer the research questions and address objectives (Saunders et al., 2015).

During the interviews (see Appendix), I used an audio recorder and took notes at the same time to ensure an accurate answer from the participants all throughout the data collection process. Interview protocol contains the interview questions and step-by-step guidance for several interviews including demographic and research questions, as well as member checking to increase the reliability and validity of the study (Yin, 2014). I used member checking to validate data and enhance trustworthiness. In order to enhance the reliability and validity, the participants have the rights to check and provide further insights on the accuracy of the findings collected (Marshall & Rossman, 2016; Noble & Smith, 2015). Therefore, participants reviewed the summaries of the interview findings during the member checking process.

Data Collection Technique

I used semistructured interviews for primary data and company commodities for the secondary data. One of the non-standardised forms of interviews is the face-to-face interview, a semistructured approach to see, hear, and feel the participants (Marshall & Rossman, 2016). Therefore, I used the face-to-face interview to see, hear, and feel the participants. An interview protocol is as a step-by-step guidance during the interview (Sutton & Austin, 2015). Thus, I utilized an interview protocol along with audio-taped recordings and handwritten notes in recording all the relevant information to the research. In contrast, the technique to find relevant secondary data is to establish the likely availability and locate the precise data (Saunders et al., 2015). I found available and qualified materials for secondary data through online databases including survey reports, newspapers, blogs, social networks, articles, and books related to the organization and download files.

Face-to-face interviews have advantages and disadvantages as a technique for data collection. Bowden and Galindo-Gonzalez (2015) identified some face-to-face interviews advantages: (a) more likely to share more stories which potentially provide additional data; (b) norm and uncontested component; (c) social cues such as paralanguage, body language, pauses, inflection, and tone; (d) control over distractions; and (e) establish rapport, asks appropriate questions, actively listen, and end the interview appropriately. Conversely, the disadvantages may include: (a) time and financial costs, (b) geographical distribution of respondents, (c) sensitive or controversial topics, (d) technology problems, (e) interviewer safety (location, time, or sexual harassment), (f) nonverbal language and cues can be misinterpreted, and (g) social pressure and personal bias (Oltmann, 2016; Yin, 2014).

I utilized a semistructured technique that do not require pilot testing as I can make corrections and address participant questions during the process of interview. Pilot studies added value and credibility to the research study as well as helps to identify unclear statements in the research protocol (Dikko, 2016). However, I used member checking to mitigate bias and develop trustworthiness. I shared a concise copy of each question and interpretation from the first interview during the follow-up and member checking interview; furthermore, I asked probing questions related to the interview then read the interpretation again to either add, change or confirm the data. Researcher may apply member checking, to assure the accuracy of the interview data and the credibility of the research findings (Birt et al., 2016; Marshall & Rossman, 2016).

Data Organization Technique

The recorded interviews, transcripts and field notes or journals were kept in a cabinet with a key lock that is not easily accessible to others. I organized the data by creating individual hard and electronic file folders labeled by the acronyms designated to the participant. I used an iPhone smartphone to record the interviews and transcribe into text before the data analysis begin, which takes an 8-hour transcribing a 45-minute audio-recorded interview (Sutton & Austin, 2015). A two-factor authentication is a way to prevent privacy infractions and breaches and maintain the participants' confidentiality towards the continuous growth of technology (Lustgarten, 2015; Quick & Choo, 2014). Therefore, I saved the data through a cloud storage called Dropbox activated with two-factor authentication.

The stored and protected data will be kept for 5 years as per the policy of Walden University, and delete all the electronic copies and destroy all the hard copies in 5-year time to provide privacy and confidentiality,. By providing confidentiality and anonymity to participants, the participants might possibly and more confidently offer rich and detailed data (Lancaster, 2016). Confidentiality is essential to maintain trust between the researcher and the participant (Novak, 2014; Saunders et al., 2015).

Data Analysis

Joslin and Muller (2016) discussed the methods of triangulation to decrease biases, increase the validity and strength of the study, and provide multiple perspectives, hence, there are five types of triangulation: (a) data triangulation, (b) investigator triangulation, (c) methodological triangulation, (d) theory triangulation, and (e) philosophical triangulation. Methodological triangulation uses multiple methods to study a research problem (Fusch & Ness, 2015). Therefore, I utilized documentation, archival records, interviews, and participant observation for methodological triangulation in validating the findings of the study.

Morse (1994) introduced a framework for data analysis based on four stages with affiliated strategies of Miles and Huberman (1994): (a) comprehending, (b) synthesizing, (c) theorizing, and (d) recontextualizing (Houghton et al., 2015). The data analysis process that I followed includes the following steps: (a) understand the interviews from the audio recordings and field notes, (b) combine the data from audio recordings and field notes to review and achieve consistency, (c) hypothesize codes and themes from the interview data, and (d) review the themes from the coded data for additional or confirmation of theme identification. I used NVivo ® software in transcribing and coding the interviews from the audio recordings. NVivo is a software to organize and facilitate the analysis and to locate the matching words or phrases from the data (Lensges, Hollensbe, & Masterson, 2016; Yin, 2014).

I utilized a constructivist approach in coding data that includes three stages: (a) initial coding, a word-by-word or line-by-line code; (b) focused coding, selecting and testing the initial coding; and (c) theoretical integration, integrating categories identified in focused coding (Holt, 2016). I wrote down notes during the interviews for mind mapping. Notes may include words, diagrams, branches, and images to build upon existing knowledge when new information is presented (Rosciano, 2015). I used the QSR NVivo in identifying themes. NVivo has a variety of search and retrieval tools called queries that enable to ask questions or test emerging themes (St. Pierre & Jackson, 2014).

Thematic analysis is one of the analytical techniques and a foundational method for qualitative analysis. The primary purpose of thematic analysis is to search for themes or patterns that occur across a data set such as interviews, observations, documents or websites that includes (a) becoming familiar with the data, (b) coding the data, (c) searching for themes and recognizing relationships, and (d) refining themes and testing propositions (Saunders et al., 2015). Inductive approach is a process to generate new theory (Neal et al., 2015). Therefore, I reviewed the field notes and audio recordings in identifying key themes. Literature review and conceptual framework help in searching for relevant themes (Al-Amer, 2014). Therefore, I kept on reading the scholarly resources of the study.

Reliability and Validity

Reliability

In a qualitative research, reliability means consistency. Reliability also associates with dependability (Leung, 2015). Korstjens and Moser (2018) defined dependability as the stability of the findings that involves participants' evaluation of the findings, interpretation, and recommendations of the study. Researcher can utilize member checking to assure the consistency of the interview data (Birt et al., 2016). Therefore, I utilized member checking and review transcripts to facilitate further investigation to the consistency of the study. Interview protocol ensures the alignment of interview questions to the research questions (Castillo-Montoya, 2016); therefore, I used an interview protocol to enhance transparency and dependability of the study.

Keep track of all the methodological decisions or data analysis in illustrating evidence and processes during the research work. An audit trail is another way to establish dependability and confirmability (El Hussein, Jakubec, & Osuji, 2015; Sarma, 2015). I utilized the data to address dependability and reliability of this study from the interviews, field notes, and examine the companies' commodities such as the company websites, social media pages, articles, and newspaper in gaining an in-depth understanding of the strategies real estate business leaders implement to attain and sustain competitive advantage to increase profitability during periods of unstable or declining markets.

Validity

In a qualitative paradigm, validity refers to the credibility, transferability, and confirmability of the research findings. Increasing the validity of qualitative outcomes develop with procedures and criteria such as the internal validity, external validity, construct validity, and reliability (Lub, 2015; Yin, 2014). Credibility also referred to as the internal validity, which builds the truth of the findings with strategies such as triangulation, member checking, prolonged engagement, and persistent observation (Korstjens & Moser, 2018). Therefore, I used member checking and follow-up interview, methodological triangulation, transcript review, and interview protocol in ensuring the credibility of the research findings and that of the participants' perspective.

Trust may be a necessity towards validity. Trustworthiness is a concept of transferability, confirmability, and credibility of the research findings (El Hussein et al., 2015). Transferability is also called external validity and is, the degree to which the results can be transferred to other contexts or settings with other respondents (Korstjens & Moser, 2018; Lub, 2015). In a qualitative study, researcher does not generalize and state that the findings are transferable unlike quantitative research (Bengtsson, 2016). Therefore, I adhered the transferability of the findings through interview protocol, documentation, and participant observation.

Confirmability may refer to the findings of the research study. Confirmability is a confirmation by other researchers, and the results of the findings and data are easily understood (Kihn & Ihantola, 2015; Korstjens & Moser, 2018). Kornbluh (2015) added that researchers may establish trustworthiness through interviews and the incorporation of participants' feedback mechanism into the data analysis process. Therefore, I applied follow-up and member checking of interviews to enhance study confirmability.

According to Fusch and Ness (2015), researcher reaches data saturation when there is enough information to replicate the study, when the ability to obtain additional new information has been attained, and when further coding is no longer feasible. Data saturation is when the researcher receives no new information or emerging themes from the same participants after several interviews (Gibbins, Bhatia, Forbes, & Reid, 2014). Methodological triangulation may also assist in reaching data saturation (Fusch, Fusch, & Ness, 2017). Therefore, I interviewed the four participants until no new data, themes, and coding to verify the data saturation. I attest the credibility, transferability, and confirmability of the research findings through data saturation.

Transition and Summary

Section 2 includes a detailed discussion of the various stages of the research project. The stages include the purpose statement, the role of the researcher, participants, the research method and design, population and sampling, ethical research, data collection instruments and techniques, data organization techniques, data analysis, and reliability and validity. The most appropriate research method and design was the qualitative multiple case study to explore the strategies real estate business leaders in Dubai, UAE implement to attain and sustain competitive advantage to increase profitability during periods of unstable or declining markets. The data collection technique was through semistructured interviews and a review of the company commodities. Section 3 includes the introduction, presentation of findings, application to professional practice, implications for social change, recommendations for action and further research, reflections, conclusion, and appendices/table of contents.

Section 3: Application to Professional Practice and Implications for Change

Introduction

The purpose of this qualitative multiple case study was to explore strategies real estate business leaders use to attain and sustain competitive advantage to increase profitability during periods of unstable or declining markets. In this section, I present my findings and discuss the themes identified. I also discuss the findings' applications to professional practice and implications for social change, and provide recommendations for action and further research, personal reflections, and my conclusions.

My findings consist of four themes to increase profitability during periods of unstable or declining markets: (a) reduce operating costs, (b) execute corporate real estate management, (c) promote corporate social responsibilities, and (d) utilize human capital. The four participants emphasized controlling costs or expenses during unstable markets. Executing corporate real estate management or increasing the value of assets added a competitive advantage for their organizations. Every participant also acknowledged the importance of promoting social responsibilities and ethical values to employees, customers, the environment, partnerships, or organizations. Furthermore, all the participants used human capital as the main source of innovation that helps them to attain and sustain an advantage over competitors.

Presentation of the Findings

The central research question for this study was: What strategies do real estate business leaders use to attain and sustain competitive advantage to increase profitability during periods of unstable or declining markets? Through interviews with real estate business leaders who successfully attained and sustained competitive advantage after the declining of markets, I identified themes. I used SWOT analysis when reviewing interview data. In what follows, I describe how the findings validate, invalidate, or extend knowledge, and tie the findings to the conceptual framework used for this study. I also reviewed available information from company websites and social media sites. Table 2 contains the summary of demographic information about the four participating real estate business leaders. The participants had a combination of 38 years of experience as real estate business leaders.

Table 2

Demographic Information Of Real Estate Business Leaders

Characteristics	Case 1	Case 2	Case 3	Case 4
Code name	P1	P2	P3	P4
Age	44	43	35	44
Country of birth	Egypt	Spain	Dubai	Syria
Highest level of educational	Bachelor's degree	Bachelor's degree	Bachelor's degree	Bachelor's degree
Length in current organization	7 years	4 years	8 years	4 years and 8 months
Years of experience as a business leader	7 years	12 years	8 years	11 years

The four themes are: (a) reduce operating costs, (b) execute corporate real estate management, (c) promote corporate social responsibilities, and (d) utilize human capital. The participants provided rich responses to the interview questions that, in combination with the conceptual framework, literature review findings, and triangulation, guided me in developing themes upon data analysis.

Theme 1: Reduce Operating Costs

The first factor that the participants used to increase profitability during periods of an unstable or declining market was to reduce or control operating costs. The four business leaders minimized the business costs including advertising or marketing, utilities, and technology. Gurel (2017) classified the variables for organizational strengths and weaknesses as marketing, research and development, management information systems, management teams, operations, finances, and human resources. According to the participants, as the companies' business leaders, they implemented the strategy of reducing the use of resources to increase profitability. P1 noted that their company combines cost reduction strategy with a positive cash flow through a stable source of profit such as property management.

Cost reductions or minimization are connected with cost leadership strategies. Prajogo (2016) observed that in a dynamic environment, product innovation strengthens business performance, but during a competitive environment, process innovation strengthens business performance through cost reduction in production and processes. Delmas and Pekovic (2015) associated cost savings during downturns with the probability of adopting resource efficiency strategies such as reducing the negative environmental impact to focus on cost leadership strategies. In addition, Bayraktar et al. (2016) suggested that innovation assists firms in reducing the cost of production and delivery but at the same time enhances quality.

P4's company recently won an international award for its marketing efforts by the Land Department of Dubai with the categories namely property consultancy website and real estate agency marketing and category of property consultancy marketing. P4 wrote an article pertaining to the award given to their company and mentioned that they specialized in marketing 24/7 leveraging the advantage of social media platforms, emails, mobile, and word of mouth. At first, they invested with property portals, but during unstable market, they had to cut down operating costs and eventually figure out that it is somehow working. P4 still use property portals for a short period although they focus on their website and social media such as Facebook, Instagram, Twitter, and LinkedIn. P2 was interviewed in a newspaper regarding the business cost factors of real estate agencies and how they face downturns in the industry. P2 responded that the firm lowers expenses by hiring competent and skilled employees only, finding enough office space, monitoring the utility expenses, and negotiating contracts with partners like maintenance, property portals, insurance, and so on.

Pulaj et al. (2015) reported that low-cost strategy generates higher profits and a successful way to achieve sustainable competitive advantage by control and reduction of costs. Likewise, Butnariu and Avasilcai (2015) found that minimizing the costs of operations leads to innovation that eventually increases the firm performance and competitive strategies. During member checking and follow-up interviews, the four participants agreed that reducing operating costs is a mandatory strategy during an unstable market. P2 added "We reduce supply expenses, we advertise less and do more of networking but taking advantage of social platforms as well". Porter's generic strategies is relevant to the theme called cost leadership. Table 3 contains the participants' statements about reducing operating costs in their companies.

Table 3

Theme: Reduce Operating Costs

Participant	Participant's Comments
P1	During a tough market, we must have attractive offer to attract tenants and specialize on few areas to focus on giving the best service. In terms of the internal factors we try to minimize our expenses as possible as we can.
P2	We give a big degree of important on costs. Keeping down all the costs during unstable market.
P3	We do maintain low level of debts and expenditures, high cash flows, and invest with or offer property management for a stable income.
P4	To drive growth we need to capitalize on augmenting the value of assets in terms of operations and controlling cost and providing exceptional service in a manner that should not jeopardize your investment value.

Theme 2: Execute Corporate Real Estate Management

All four business leaders agreed on executing corporate real estate management (CREM) in attaining and sustaining competitive advantage to increase profitability during an unstable market. Because their organizations involve property management, facilities management, and acquisition of properties, the participants adopted the CREM strategy in which the management aligns the corporate real estate portfolio (CRE) and services to the core business. Oladokun and Aluko (2015) enumerated the seven strategies of CRE: (a) increasing the value of assets, (b) promoting marketing and sales, (c) increasing innovation, (d) increase employee satisfaction, (e) increase productivity, (f) increase flexibility, and (g) reducing cost. P1 explained "The number one asset of any organizations are the employees, so when you have satisfied employees that is equivalent to productivity towards sales, marketing, and innovation. In addition, flexibility automatically occurs with the uncertainties of the market and economy".

Apart from the interview data, the information from the participating companies' websites verified the execute corporate real estate management theme. On P3's website, the company covers every aspect in the real estate sector to increase the value of assets including property management, property investment, property maintenance, business consultancy, and so on. Furthermore, the company is attentive to the details of marketing and sales of real estate. P1's company's website reports its core values include increasing employee's satisfaction through respect, teamwork, honesty, communication, and leadership in order to increase productivity and flexibility. P2's company website reports that the company increases innovation using a high-tech equipped workforce and operating systems.

The execute corporate real estate management theme was evident in Smeets, Ploumen, and Meulenbroek (2015) study pertaining to the tasks of CREM in the real estate lifecycle, particularly on ensuring the availability of acquisition or leasing, keeping facility management and dispositions. Thus, CREM's components influence the competitive advantage of the organization including organizational structure, centralization, sourcing, process management, and company culture (Smeets et al., 2015). The theme aligns with the SWOT analysis as an internal aspect of strengths and weaknesses and an organizational component towards the management and process of a business. Czajkowska (2016) examined the process and management as part of building strengths and minimizing weaknesses. Thus, CREM is a possible process that management could implement to attain and sustain competitive advantage. Table 4 contains the participants' statements on executing CREM in their companies.

Table 4

Theme: Execute Corporate Real Estate Management

Participant	Participant's Comments
P1	Apart from one of our main strategy which is the cost reduction, we also try our best on increasing the value of our assets by keeping high and stable returns from the 5 full buildings we are exclusively managing. At the same time, we value our employees as they play a very important role to make our organization not just profitable but sustainable as well. We can't deny that the number one asset of any organizations is the employees, so when you have satisfied employees that is equivalent to productivity and flexibility especially during the uncertainties of the market and economy.
P2	We categorize our clients and the rest of stakeholders as intangible assets that's one way we increase our value of assets. We value their trusts in our capabilities so we provide what is entrusted to us. We also built a relationship and collaborations with developers, bank & mortgage brokerage firms, maintenance and so forth. Through this, we do not only increase the value of our assets and at the same time it is a low-cost operation or strategy to increase market and sales.
P3	I would say that we invested a lot in marketing and sales during the first year of our business. We always try to be on top of property portals. We did advertisements on social platforms, emails, and word of mouth. We also promote employee's satisfaction to motivate them to be productive and innovative. In the long run, we hire and provide extensive training to the people that are flexible enough to be one of the assets of our company.
P4	To be more competitive in the market, we take innovation into higher level using high-tech equipped work force and operating systems like geo-location map. Our diversified and highly qualified team commits an attention to detail to the marketing and sales of properties for our investors, landlords, and tenants. As for our assets, the employees, we increase their satisfactions just as much as our clients to keep them productive and motivated.

All the participants mentioned that their strategic management in developing competitive advantage is based on one or more of the following factors: the value of assets, marketing and sales, innovation, employees' satisfaction, productivity, flexibility, and cost reduction. The second theme was influenced by the CRE because these are the main strategies that the CREM department may choose from. Furthermore, CREM's main tasks involve (a) ensuring availability of CRE such as acquisition, leasing, and development; (b) keeping CREM operational through facility management; and (c) its dispositions like rental administration or disposal (Smeets et al., 2015).

Theme 3: Promote Corporate Social Responsibility

Every participant acknowledged the positive impact of corporate social responsibility (CSR) towards competitive advantage. CSR is based on ethical values that involve employees, customers, and environment which evolved into business ethics, citizenship, and stakeholder management (Carroll, 2015). The methodological triangulation of the interview data and the information from the participant's company websites and social platforms verified the theme through their vision statements integrated with high ethical standards with core values such as integrity, respect, commitment, honesty, reliability, and efficiency.

In my examination of the participating companies' websites, I identified statements such as to fulfill our company vision, we will incorporate professionalism, high ethical standards, and innovative business practices and spares no efforts to create every possible chance to bring prosperity, happiness, and serenity within a professional, ethical, and customer satisfaction targeted platform. According to P1, they do what is right, fair, ethical, and prioritize honesty and integrity above all. While P4 stated and indicated on their website that they take great pride in providing top-notch services while keeping integrity as a forefront in everything they do.

Promote corporate social responsibility theme was relevant to Moczadlo (2015) findings that CSR is a long-term business strategy considering the economic, social, and environmental factors with ethical human rights as a core element for competitive advantage. Saedi et al. (2015) added that CSR has a positive association with firm's performance including monetary performance, personal commitment, and corporate integrity. Ağan et al. (2016) studied the influence of CSR towards environmental supplier development to a firm's financial performance and competitive advantage. Conversely, Kwarteng et al. (2016) combined the triple bottom line (social, environmental and financial factors) along with CSR and stakeholder theory to sustain competitive advantage while De Guimarães et al. (2017) explored the organizational performance and competitive advantage through environmental sustainability and CSR. The theme aligns with the SWOT analysis as an external aspect of opportunities and threats and an environmental component pertaining to the society. Thus, CSR is an ethical approach towards social, economic, and environmental factors, that could be a core element of competitive advantage. Table 5 contains the participant's statements on promoting corporate social responsibility in their respective companies.

Table 5

Theme: Promote Corporate Social Responsibility

Participant	Participant's Comments
P1	Integrity is the main factor in keeping the business surviving in this tough time in Dubai. I started with nothing in Dubai (as a security guard) but since I build a good relationship with my clients, they have trusted me and referred to other clients, till I grow my business as it is now.
P2	Social factors are very important as well. We make sure that our strategies are ethically right and fair to our people, customers, organizations, and the environment. We focus on social factors by creating a good reputation on the market and offer a good relationship.
P3	Social factors are very important at all times in any corporate culture and maintaining a very high standard of ethics and to all businesses it is very important. For example, how unethical companies end up, they usually do not end up well. In addition, maintaining a high standard of ethics elevates the positive in society and shows the companies cares to the people.
P4	Social responsibility has become increasingly important to companies over the last several years and more and more companies are incorporating social responsibility into their overall business strategy. It is a form of giving back to the community. It improves a company's image, builds its brand and loyalty for sure.

Theme 4: Utilize Human Capital

The four business leaders in the real estate industry agreed that utilizing human capital established edge over competitors. Czajkowska (2016) identified the internal factors of the strengths and weaknesses of an organization are the customer, employees, capabilities, resources, and process. According to Todericiu and Stanit (2015), human capital refers to the employee's skills, expertise, knowledge, competencies, and know-how. Sikora et al. (2016) reported the effectiveness of human capital along with resource-based theory into a long-term competitive advantage.

The participants acknowledged the importance of employees and their capabilities as the main resource during a crucial performance of their organizations. P1 mentioned on their website that the company's ongoing success and its high reputation in the property industry lie on the unique talent and hard work of their team. P2 explained that their company survives during unstable markets through their people. P2 added that they make sure that each and every employee are hands-on and extending their services towards new and existing customers. P3 shared that investing in the people first and foremost will enable the company's success. P4 added that their experts help the clients not just to sell but to give what they only need.

Utilize human capital theme was applied in Prajogo and Oke (2016) examination that human capital has a positive effect on competitive advantage as intangible resources because capabilities, knowledge, and skills are rare; hence, valuable, non-substitutable, and hard to imitate. Delery and Roumpi (2017) extended the knowledge of human capital to human resource management practices and activities that contribute to a firm's sustainable competitive advantage. Thus, HRM activities include investment and intensive training, selective staffing, performance appraisals, team building, and firm- specific skills while HRM practices consist of firm specify, social complexity, and causal ambiguity (Delery & Roumpi, 2017). The theme aligns with the SWOT analysis as strengths and weaknesses of a business, specifically the employees, capabilities, and resources. Table 6 contains the participant's statements on utilizing human capital in their respective companies.

Table 6

Theme: Utilize Human Capital

Participant	Participant's Comments
P1	Human capital is the most vital part of innovation as they are liable for the ideas, plans, strategies, implementation and so forth. So, it is very important especially with our kind of business. At the end of the day, real estate business is a trust and service game.
P2	Our employee's skills and capabilities serve as our key to innovative business practices. We rely on our people's knowledge to create an advantage over our competitors either it's through advertisements or services.
P3	Nothing beats human creativity and innovation, not even computers no matter how innovative and how great they become. Investing in human resources at all time will always have better results than investing in else. It doesn't mean that a company should invest in IT, it's very important to invest in IT, but investing in the people first and foremost will enable the company's success.
P4	I believe the most valuable part of your company is the people or the human capital that any plans to move your business forward have to start there.

Application to Professional Practice

The result of this study could prove valuable to current and future leaders of real estate businesses for using strategies to attain and sustain competitive advantage to increase profitability during periods of unstable or declining markets. Real estate business leaders may enhance their firm performance by applying the findings of the study. The findings include four themes: (a) reduce operating costs, (b) execute corporate real estate management, (c) promote corporate social responsibility, and (d) utilize human capital. The findings and conclusions can help benefit real estate business leaders mitigate loss of profits or bankruptcy. SWOT analysis influences the strategic planning of an organization towards competitive advantage and aids on decision-making to boost strengths, eliminate weaknesses, embrace opportunities, and act on threats of a business including the industry (Abdel-Basset, 2018). Therefore, real estate business leaders could use 'utilize human capital theme' as one of the major strengths of a business and source in forming a team who could 'execute the corporate real estate management theme' and help on solving environmental opportunities and threats such as societal factors through 'promoting social responsibilities theme'. In Porter's Generic Strategies, applying a cost leadership and its method called cost reductions or minimization during downturn market conditions promotes higher profits and lower business costs factors (Pulaj et al., 2015). Therefore, real estate business leaders may apply 'reducing operating costs theme' along with the application of 'execute corporate real estate management theme' because these are both organizational strengths and weaknesses of a business. In general, medium-sized real estate businesses do not obtain competent competitive advantage strategies during unstable markets. Current and future real estate industry business leaders could adopt and use the strategies to attain and sustain competitive advantage during unstable markets.

Implications for Social Change

The result of this study could help in enhancing strategic management and business performance of real estate businesses. Dubai is not the capital of U.A.E and an oil-dependent country; however, the real estate sector is one of the highest contributors among non-oil industry to increase the UAE's GDP during financial crisis. Therefore, the growth and profitability of real estate companies in Dubai are both important and beneficial to the individuals and communities. The lack of knowledge on competitive advantage strategies may cause loss of profits or bankruptcy. The result of this study could create a difference on strategies in attaining and sustaining competitive advantage to increase profitability during unstable markets. Thus, real estate business leaders can study and execute a goal into plans in accordance to the SWOT factors of their organizations with the influence of strategic management.

A sustainable and profitable real estate company may create jobs for individuals, income for the community, growth for organizations and affiliated industries, promotion of culture, good economy for the society, and introduce the local scene into a foreign environment. Furthermore, real estate in Dubai represents extraordinary value for money for investors (Sundarakani, 2017). The findings from this study could contribute to social change by sharing to business leaders the competitive advantage strategies to increase profitability during a local or global financial crisis.

Recommendations for Action

The purpose of this qualitative multiple case study was to explore strategies that the real estate industry business leaders use to attain and sustain competitive advantage to increase profitability during unstable markets. Based on the findings of this study, I propose several actions that the current and future real estate business leaders can take to increase profitability during local or global financial crisis. The business leaders need to understand the four key issues for influencing their success: (a) reduce operating costs, (b) execute corporate real estate management, (c) promote corporate social responsibility, and (d) utilize human capital.

First, finance or accounting department of real estate companies should apply cost reductions to make an efficient operating cost, save financial resources, and reduce time-consuming activities. Reducing the costs may not affect the quality of services if business leaders take advantage of the technology and invest on people. Second, top management should adopt corporate real estate strategies to promote marketing and sales, reduce costs, and to increase the value of assets, innovation, employee satisfaction, productivity, flexibility. Oladokun and Aluko (2015) concluded that corporate real estate management is being used in Nigeria for over 69% among private companies, public organizations or government sector. Third, employees should promote corporate social responsibility to build a good reputation in the market and corporate integrity. The CSR started for individual rights and eventually evolved into business ethics, corporate citizenship, sustainability, and stakeholder engagement (Carroll, 2015). Fourth, business leaders should utilize human capital because skills and knowledge are rare, valuable, non-substitutable, and difficult to imitate. Prajogo and Oke (2016) confirmed the positive effect of human capital on competitive advantage and business performance as an asset towards new services, processes, technologies, and methods; hence, the capabilities of human are intangible resources of a firm. I intend to publish the study and take advantage of opportunities to share findings with business leaders in the real estate industry, colleges and universities, and business forums where business leaders discuss competitive advantage strategies to increase profitability during unstable markets.

Recommendations for Further Research

I conducted a qualitative multiple case study on the strategies that medium-sized real estate industry business leaders use to attain and sustain competitive advantage to increase profitability during unstable markets. The population for this study consisted of four cases in Dubai, U.A.E., and the small size is one of the limitations of this study. Thus, the findings from this study may not be generalizable to other industries. Future researchers should consider doing a deeper study between human capital and human resources to understand the difference of letting the individuals contribute more than one's role in an organization and working based only on their job titles and functions; hence, people are individuals that need to be studied, controlled, and defined. In addition, future researchers can use the quantitative methodology on a larger population and develop a hypothesis to test the correlation between competitive advantage and the themes identified in this study.

Reflections

In this study, I explored the strategies that real estate business leaders use to attain and sustain competitive advantage to increase profitability during unstable markets. Having this opportunity to conduct the research and find potential solutions to the business problems, I learned the lessons and knowledge that I could not get from any books. I acquired skills that I could develop and gathered an abundance of information from the experiences of the business leaders.

Upon approaching the data collection, I underestimated the method of obtaining the targeted participants. Over 50-60% of the business leaders that I contacted did not reply to the invitation letter that I sent thru email, while some of them have personal problems that they had to prioritize and decided to drop out. Among the participants who willingly accepted the invitation, I provided enough period to understand the process and at their most convenient time. I informed them that there are methods that could be a little repetitive particularly the transcript review and member checking process. I also instructed them about the interview protocol as a step by step guide to avoid confusions regarding the questions and flow; hence, I briefed them that the follow-up questions for the final interview depend on their initial answers. Transcribing the audios was also challenging and time-consuming.

The participants imparted strategies that real estate business leaders could use to attain and sustain competitive advantage to increase profitability during unstable markets. Having the one-on-one interaction between the knowledgeable and well-experienced business leaders motivated me in so many ways as a leader and an individual. I learned that one's own experience is not the only teacher that could teach us, other's experience does too.

Conclusions

Competitive advantage is needed either on dynamic, mature or competitive environment. Strategic management is one of the keys to attain and sustain competitive advantage through identifying the strengths, weaknesses, opportunities, and threats factors to create such strategy (Dyer et al., 2016). The lack of competitive advantage of a business may result in loss of profits and worse, into a bankruptcy especially during a local or global financial crisis. Thus, real estate business leaders must give time to identify the right strategies based on their customers, employees, resources, and capabilities including social, environmental, and financial factors. In particular, real estate business leaders should adopt corporate real estate strategies because it engages with the most important aspects of the business; hence, from having a realistic budget and sufficient funds, to overspending on marketing, to inadequate knowledge towards human capital, to being innovative but ignorant to rules and regulations, and incompetent management of assets.

References

Abdel-Basset, M., Mohamed, M., & Smarandache, F. (2018). An extension of

Neutrosophic AHP-SWOT analysis for strategic planning and decision-making.

Symmetry, 10, 116-134. doi:10.3390/sym10040116

Ağan, Y., Kuzey, C., Acar, M. F., & Açıkgöz, A. (2016). The relationships between

corporate social responsibility, environmental supplier development, and firm

performance. *Journal of Cleaner Production, 112*, 1872-1881.

doi:10.1016/j.jclepro.2014.08.090

Aghazadeh, H. (2015). Strategic marketing management: Achieving superior business

performance through intelligent marketing strategy. *Procedia Social and

Behavioral Sciences, 207,* 125-134. doi:10.1016/j.sbspro.2015.10.161

Ahmad, A. (2015). Business intelligence for sustainable competitive advantage. In

Quaddus, M., & Woodside, Arch. (Ed). *Sustaining Competitive Advantage Via

Business Intelligence, Knowledge Management, and System Dynamics, 22*, 3-220.

doi:10.1108/s1069-09642015000022b005

Ahmed, A. Z. E. (2015). The role of diversification strategies in the economic

development for oil-depended countries the case of UAE. *The Business &

Management Review, 6*, 207-216. Retrieved from http://www.abrmr.com/

Al-Amer, R., Ramjan, L., Glew, P., Darwish, M., & Salamonson, Y. (2014). Translation

of interviews from a source language to a target language: Examining issues in

cross-cultural health care research. *Journal of Clinical Nursing, 24*, 1151-1162.

doi:10.1111/jocn.12681

Alawadi, K. (2017). Rethinking Dubai's urbanism: Generating sustainable form-based urban design strategies for an integrated neighborhood. *Cities, 60*, 353-366. doi:10.1016/j.cities.2016.10.012

Albrecht, S., Bakker, A., Gruman, J., Macey, W., & Saks, A. (2015). Employee engagement, human resource management practices and competitive advantage: An integrated approach. *Journal of Organizational Effectiveness: People and Performance, 2*, 7-35. doi:10.1108/JOEPP-08-2014-0042

Aldairi, J. S., Khan, M. K., & Munive-Hernandez, J. E. (2016). A hybrid knowledge-based lean six sigma maintenance system for sustainable buildings. In Ao S., Yang GC., Gelman L. (Eds) *Transactions on Engineering Technologies*, 355-369. Gateway East, Singapore: Springer Nature. doi:10.1007/978-981-10-1088-0_27

Al Faris, A., & Soto, R. (2016). *The economy of Dubai*. New York, NY: Oxford University Press. doi:10.1093/acprof:oso/9780198758389.001.0001

Alonso-Almeida, M., Bremser, K., & Llach, J. (2015). Proactive and reactive strategies deployed by restaurants in times of crisis. *International Journal of Contemporary Hospitality Management, 27*, 1641-1661. doi:10.1108/ijchm-03-2014-0117

Amiri, N. S., Shirkavand, S., Chalak, M., & Rezaeei, N. (2017). Competitive intelligence and developing sustainable competitive advantage. *Ad-minister, 30*, 173-194. doi:10.17230/ad-minister.30.9

Anastasia, N., & Suwitro, A. (2015). The rational and irrational factors underlying property buying behavior. *Journal of Economics and Behavioral Studies, 7*, 183-191. Retrieved from https://ifrnd.org/

Antonakis, J., Bastardoz, N., Liu, Y., & Schriesheim, C. A. (2014). What makes articles highly cited? *The Leadership Quarterly, 25,* 152-179. doi:10.1016/j.leaqua.2013.10.014

Ashrafi, R., & Mueller, J. (2015). Delineating it resources and capabilities to obtain competitive advantage and improve firm performance. *Information Systems Management, 32,* 15-38. doi:10.1080/10580530.2015.983016

Aykan, E. (2017). Gaining a competitive advantage through green human resource management. In Emeagwali, L. *Corporate Governance and Strategic Decision Making,* 159-176. London, United Kingdom: Intech. doi:10.5772/intechopen.69703

Aziz, N. N. A., & Samad, S. (2016). Innovation and competitive advantage: Moderating effects of firm age in foods manufacturing SMEs in Malaysia. *Procedia Economics and Finance, 35,* 256-266. doi:10.1016/S2212-5671(16)00032-0

Bajpai, A., & Bhalchandra, P. (2015). Rational & irrational factors affecting real estate buying behavior of different nationalities with special reference of Dubai: A survey. *International Journal of Business Quantitative Economics and Applied Management Research, 2*(4), 55-67. Retrieved from http://ijbemr.com/

Balashova, E., & Gromova, E. (2016). Resource-based view as a perspective management model in Russian reality. *Problems and Perspectives in Management, 14,* 325-330. doi:10.21511/ppm.14(2-2).2016.08

Bayraktar, C. A., Hancerliogullari, G., Cetinguc, B., & Calisir, F. (2016). Competitive strategies, innovation, and firm performance: An empirical study in a developing economy environment. *Technology Analysis & Strategic Management, 29*(1), 38-52. doi:10.1080/09537325.2016.1194973

Belenzon, S., & Tsolmon, U. (2015). Market frictions and the competitive advantage of internal labor markets. *Strategic Management Journal, 37*, 1280-1303. doi:10.1002/smj.2395

Bellner, B. W., & MacLean, D. (2015). Dynamic managerial capabilities and competitive advantage. *Strategic Management Quarterly, 3*(3), 1-23. doi:10.15640/smq.v3n3a1

Bengtsson, M. (2016). How to plan and perform a qualitative study using content analysis. *NursingPlus Open, 2*, 8-14. doi:10.1016/j.npls.2016.01.001

Birt, L., Scott, S., Cavers, D., Campbell, C., & Walter, F. (2016). Member checking: A tool to enhance trustworthiness or merely a nod to validation? *Qualitative Health Research, 26,* 1802-1811. doi:10.1177/1049732316654870

Bodolica, V., Spraggon, M., & Shahid, A. (2018). Strategic adaptation to environmental jolts: An analysis of corporate resilience in the property development sector in Dubai. *Middle East J. of Management, 5*(1), 1. doi:10.1504/mejm.2018.088724

Bowden, C., & Galindo-Gonzalez, S. (2015). Interviewing when you're not face-to-face: The use of email interviews in a phenomenological study. *International Journal of Doctoral Studies, 10*, 79-92. doi:10.28945/2104

Brem, A., Maier, M., & Wimschneider, C. (2016). Competitive advantage through innovation: The case of Nespresso. *European Journal of Innovation Management, 19*, 133-148. doi:10.1108/EJIM-05-2014-0055

Bustinza, O., Bigdeli, A. Z., Baines, T., & Elliot, C. (2015). Importance of organizational structure and value chain position. *Research Technology Management, 58*(5), 53-60. doi:10.5437/08956308X5805354

Butnariu, A., & Avasilcai, S. (2015). The influence of the environmental organizational capabilities on the competitive advantage. *Annals of the Oradea University Fascicle of Management and Technological Engineering, 24*(1), 75-78. doi:10.15660/auofmte.2015-1.3092

Caldwell, C., Licona, B., & Floyd, L. A. (2015). Internal marketing to achieve competitive advantage. *International Business and Management, 10*, 1-8. doi:10.3968/6298

Carroll, A. (2015). Corporate social responsibility: The centerpiece of competing and complementary frameworks. *Organizational Dynamics, 44*(2), 87-96. Retrieved from https://www.elsevier.com/

Castillo-Montoya, M. (2016). Preparing for interview research: The interview protocol refinement framework. *The Qualitative Report, 21*, 811-831. Retrieved from https://nsuworks.nova.edu/

Cayir Ervural, B., Zaim, S., Demirel, O. F., Aydin, Z., & Delen, D. (2018). An ANP and fuzzy TOPSIS-based SWOT analysis for Turkey's energy planning. *Renewable and Sustainable Energy Reviews, 82*, 1538-1550. doi:10.1016/j.rser.2017.06.095

Cengel, O., & Oztek, Y. (2014). Competitive marketing strategies in the Turkish real estate and a research in the sector. *AJIT-e Online Academic Journal of Information Technology, 5*(17), 67-87. doi:10.5824/1309-1581.2014.4.005.x

Chahal, H., & Bakshi, P. (2015). Examining intellectual capital and competitive

    advantage relationship: Role of innovation and organizational learning.

    International Journal of Bank Marketing, 33, 376-399.

    doi:10.1108/IJBM-07-2013-0069

Chartres, L. (2014). The linkage between competitive and operational advantage and

    entrepreneurship within Australian real estate franchises. *Pacific Rim Property*

    Research Journal, 20, 171-185. doi:10.1080/14445921.2014.11104394

Chatzoglou, P., & Chatzoudes, D. (2018). The role of innovation in building competitive

    advantages: An empirical investigation. *European Journal of Innovation*

    Management, 21(1), 44-69. doi:10.1108/EJIM-02-2017-0015

Chen, M. (2014). SWOT analysis and strategies to support college physical education

    through distance education. *World Transactions on Engineering and Technology*

    Education, 12, 671-674. Retrieved from www.wiete.com.au

Chen, S. P., & Mykletun, R. J. (2015). Beyond post-downsizing organizational injustice

    and counterproductive work behaviors: Antecedents and consequences of learnt

    helplessness. *International Journal of Business and Management, 10*(6), 1-14.

    doi:10.5539/ijbm.v10n6p1

Chuang, M.Y., Chen, C.J., & Lin, M. J. (2016). The impact of social capital on

    competitive advantage. *Management Decision, 54*, 1443-1463.

    doi:10.1108/md-11-2015-0485

Cleary, M., Horsfall, J., & Hayter, M. (2014). Data collection and sampling in qualitative

    research: does size matter? *Journal of Advanced Nursing, 70*, 473-475.

doi:10.1111/jan.12163

Coccia, M. (2016). Sources of technological innovation: Radical and incremental innovation problem-driven to support competitive advantage of firms. *Technology Analysis & Strategic Management, 29*, 1048-1061. doi:10.1080/09537325.2016.1268682

Coff, R., & Raffiee, J. (2015). Toward a theory of perceived firm-specific human capital. *Academy of Management Perspectives, 29*, 326-341. doi:10.5465/amp.2014.0112

Colvin, R. M., Witt, G. B., & Lacey, J. (2016). Approaches to identifying stakeholders in environmental management: Insights from practitioners to go beyond the usual suspects. *Land Use Policy, 52*, 266-276. doi:10.1016/j.landusepol.2015.12.032

Connelly, L. M. (2014). Ethical considerations in research studies. *MEDSURG Nursing, 23*(1), 54-55. Retrieved from www.medsurgnursing.net

Czajkowska, A. (2016). SWOT analysis application for indications of the strategy action chosen enterprise in the construction sector. *Production Engineering Archives, 10*, 33-37. Retrieved from www.qpij.pl

Daleure, G. (2016). *Emiratization in the UAE labor market: Opportunities and challenges*. Gateway East, Singapore: Springer Nature.

Dangelico, R., & Pontrandolfo, P. (2015). Being green and competitive: The impact of environmental actions and collaborations on firm performance. *Business Strategy and the Environment, 24*, 413-430. doi:10.1002/bse.1828

Davis, P. (2017). How to realize strategy and build competitive advantage through your people: Increase resource heterogeneity; decrease resource mobility. *Human Resource Management International Digest, 25*(4), 7-9. doi:10.1108/HRMID-01-2017-0019

De Guimarães, J. C. F., Andréa Severo, E., & De Vasconcelos, C. R. M. (2017). Sustainable competitive advantage: A survey of companies in Southern Brazil. *Brazilian Business Review, 14*, 352-367. doi:10.15728/bbr.2017.14.3.6

Delery, J. E., & Roumpi, D. (2017). Strategic human resource management, human capital and competitive advantage: Is the field going in circles? *Human Resource Management Journal, 27*(1), 1-21. doi:10.1111/1748-8583.12137

Delmas, M. A., & Pekovic, S. (2015). Resource efficiency strategies and market conditions. *Long Range Planning, 48*(2), 80-94. doi:10.1016/j.lrp.2013.08.014

Deloitte. (2018). *Middle East real estate predictions Dubai 2018*. Retrieved from https://www2.deloitte.com/

Dereli, D. D. (2015). Innovation management in global competition and competitive advantage. *Procedia Social and Behavioral Sciences, 195*, 1365-1370. doi:10.1016/j.sbspro.2015.06.323

Dikko, M. (2016). Establishing construct validity and reliability: Pilot testing of a qualitative interview for research in takaful (Islamic insurance). *The Qualitative Report, 21*, 521-528. Retrieved from https://nsuworks.nova.edu/

Dyer, J. H., Godfrey, P., Jensen, R., & Bryce, D. (2016). *Strategic management: Concepts and tools for creating real world strategy.* Hoboken, NJ: John Wiley & Sons.

El Hussein, M., Jakubec, S. L., & Osuji, J. (2015). Assessing the FACTS: A Mnemonic for teaching and learning the rapid assessment of rigor in qualitative research studies. *The Qualitative Report, 20*, 1182-1184. Retrieved from https://nsuworks.nova.edu/tqr/vol20/iss8/3

Eloranta, V., & Turunen, T. (2015). Seeking competitive advantage with service infusion: A systematic literature review. *Journal of Service Management, 26*, 394-425. doi:10.1108/JOSM-12-2013-0359

Etikan, I. (2016). Comparison of convenience sampling and purposive sampling. *American Journal of Theoretical and Applied Statistics, 5*(1), 1-4. doi:10.11648/j.ajtas.20160501.11

Felin, T., & Powell, T. C. (2016). Designing organizations for dynamic capabilities. *California Management Review, 58*(4), 78-96. doi:10.1525/cmr.2016.58.4.78

Friesen, P., Kearns, L., Redman, B., & Caplan, A. L. (2017). Rethinking the Belmont report? *The American Journal of Bioethics, 17*(7), 15-21. doi:10.1080/15265161.2017.1329482

Fusch, P. I., Fusch, G. E., & Ness, L. R. (2017). How to conduct a mini-ethnographic case study: A guide for novice researchers. *The Qualitative Report, 22*, 923-941. Retrieved from https://nsuworks.nova.edu/

Fusch, P. I., & Ness, L. R. (2015). Are we there yet? Data saturation in qualitative

    research. *The Qualitative Report, 20*, 1408-1416. Retrieved from

    https://nsuworks.nova.edu/

Gabrielsson, M., Seppälä, T., & Gabrielsson, P. (2016). Realizing a hybrid competitive

    strategy and achieving superior financial performance while internationalizing in

    the high-technology market. *Industrial Marketing Management, 54*, 141-153.

    doi:10.1016/j.indmarman.2015.07.001

Gentles, S. J., Charles, C., Ploeg, J., & McKibbon, K. (2015). Sampling in qualitative

    research: Insights from an overview of the methods literature. *The Qualitative*

    Report, 20, 1772-1789. Retrieved from https://nsuworks.nova.edu/

Gibbins, J., Bhatia, R., Forbes, K., & Reid, C. M. (2014). What do patients with advanced

    incurable cancer want from the management of their pain? A qualitative study.

    Palliative Medicine, 28(1), 71-78. doi:10.1177/0269216313486310

Giniuniene, J., & Jurksiene, L. (2015). Dynamic capabilities, innovation and

    organizational learning: interrelations and impact on firm performance. *Procedia*

    Social and Behavioral Sciences, 213, 985-991. doi:10.1016/j.sbspro.2015.11.515

Giurgiu, C., & Borza, A. (2015). Strategy from conceptualization to competitive

    advantage. *Annals of the University of Oradea, Economic Science Series, 24*,

    1109-1119. Retrieved from https://doaj.org/

Gould, A. M., & Desjardins, G. (2015). A spring-clean of Michael Porter's attic.

    Competitiveness Review, 25, 310-323. doi:10.1108/cr-04-2014-0008

Grady, C. (2015). Enduring and emerging challenges of informed consent. *New England Journal of Medicine, 372*, 855-862. doi:10.1056/nejmra1411250

Grady, C. (2015). Institutional Review Boards. *Chest, 148*, 1148-1155. doi:10.1378/chest.15-0706

Greenwood, M., Kendrick, T., Davies, H., & Gill, F. J. (2017). Hearing voices: Comparing two methods for analysis of focus group data. *Applied Nursing Research, 35*, 90-93. doi:10.1016/j.apnr.2017.02.024

Gregory, A., Whittaker, J., & Yan, X. (2016). Corporate social performance, competitive advantage, earnings persistence and firm value. *Journal of Business Finance & Accounting, 43*(1-2), 3-30. doi:10.1111/jbfa.12182

Griga, W. (2017). *Managing inpatriation: Making assignments more effective.* Wiesbaden, Germany: Springer Gabler. doi:10.1007/978-3-658-18829-0

Grošelj, P., & Zadnik Stirn, L. (2015). The environmental management problem of Pohorje, Slovenia: A new group approach within ANP - SWOT framework. *Journal of Environmental Management, 161*, 106-112. doi:10.1016/j.jenvman.2015.06.038

Gupta, P. (2017). Eastern Housing Limited - Marketing strategies of real estate company in Bangladesh. *Vision: The Journal of Business Perspective, 21*(1), 97-100. doi:10.1177/0972262916686629

Gurel, E. (2017). SWOT analysis: A theoretical review. *The Journal of International Social Research, 10,* 994-1006. doi:10.17719/jisr.2017.1832

Haegele, J. A., & Hodge, S. R. (2015). Quantitative methodology: A guide for emerging physical education and adapted physical education researchers. *The Physical Educator, 72*(5), 59-75. doi:10.18666/tpe-2015-v72-i5-6133

Hafeez, K., Foroudi, P., Dinnie, K., Nguyen, B., & Parahoo, S. K. (2016). The role of place branding and image in the development of sectoral clusters: The case of Dubai. *Journal of Brand Management, 23*, 383-402. doi:10.1057/bm.2016.18

Hakkak, M., & Ghodsi, M. (2015). Development of a sustainable competitive advantage model based on balanced scorecard. *International Journal of Asian Social Science, 5*, 298-308. doi:10.18488/journal.1/2015.5.5/1.5.298.308

Hales, G., & Mclarney, C. (2017). Uber's competitive advantage vis-a-vis Porter's generic strategies. *IUP Journal of Management Research, 16*(4), 7-22. Retrieved from http://www.iupindia.in/

Harrigan, K. (2017). Strategic flexibility and competitive advantage. *Oxford Research Encyclopedia of Business and Management.* doi:10.1093/acrefore/9780190224851.013.2

Higgs M., & Dulewicz V. (2016). Leading with Emotional Intelligence. Cham, Switzerland: Palgrave Macmillan. doi:10.1007/978-3-319-32637-5_6

Holt, N. (2016), Doing grounded theory in sport and exercise. In Smith, B., & Sparkes, A. *Routledge Handbook of Qualitative Research in Sport and Exercise*, 24-36. London, UK: Routledge. doi:10.4324/9781315762012.ch3

Houghton, C., Murphy, K., Shaw, D., & Casey, D. (2015). Qualitative case study data analysis: An example from practice. *Nurse Researcher, 22*(5), 8-12. doi:10.7748/nr.22.5.8.e1307

Huang, K.F., Dyerson, R., Wu, L.Y., & Harindranath, G. (2015). From temporary competitive advantage to sustainable competitive advantage. *British Journal of Management, 26*, 617-636. doi:10.1111/1467-8551.12104

Humphrey, A. (2005). SWOT analysis for management consulting. *SRI Alumni Newsletter*. SRI International, United States.

Huston, S., Lahbash, E. A., & Parsa, A. (2015). Investigating the UAE Residential Valuation System: A framework for analysis. *World Academy of Science, Engineering and Technology, International Journal of Social, Behavioral, Educational, Economic, Business and Industrial Engineering, 9*, 765-768. doi:10.2139/ssrn.2553738

Ibrahim, W. E. (2018). Foreigners' real estate property in United Arab Emirates: Comparative study. *Books of policy and law, 18*, 1-18. doi:10.12816/0046002

Jadalhaq, I. M. (2017). Fundamentals of the real estate legislative system and its impact on sustainable development: Dubai case study. *Arab Law Quarterly, 31*, 388-410. doi:10.1163/15730255-12314030

Jahanshahi, A. A., Nawaser, K., Eizi, N., & Etemadi, M. (2015). The role of real options thinking in achieving sustainable competitive advantage for SMEs. *Global Business and Organizational Excellence, 35*(1), 35-44. doi:10.1002/joe.21643

Jensen, H.R. (2015). Creating and maintaining sustainable relationships with customers in consumer markets. In Sidin S., & Manrai A. (Ed), *Proceedings of the 1997 World Marketing Congress. Developments in Marketing Science: Proceedings of the Academy of Marketing Science*, 631-635. Cham, Switzerland: Springer. doi:10.1007/978-3-319-17320-7_158

Jiang, J. Y., & Liu, C. W. (2015). High performance work systems and organizational effectiveness: The mediating role of social capital. *Human Resource Management Review, 25*, 126-137. doi:10.1016/j.hrmr.2014.09.001

Joslin, R., & Müller, R. (2016). Identifying interesting project phenomena using philosophical and methodological triangulation. *International Journal of Project Management, 34*, 1043-1056. doi:10.1016/j.ijproman.2016.05.005

Judkins-Cohn, T. M., Kielwasser-Withrow, K., Owen, M., & Ward, J. (2014). Ethical principles of informed consent: Exploring nurses' dual role of care provider and researcher. *The Journal of Continuing Education in Nursing, 45*(1), 35-42. doi:10.3928/00220124-20131223-03

Kaiser, M. G., El Arbi, F., & Ahlemann, F. (2015). Successful project portfolio management beyond project selection techniques: Understanding the role of structural alignment. *International Journal of Project Management, 33*, 126-139. doi:10.1016/j.ijproman.2014.03.002

Kallio, H., Pietilä, A.-M., Johnson, M., & Kangasniemi, M. (2016). Systematic methodological review: developing a framework for a qualitative semistructured interview guide. *Journal of Advanced Nursing, 72*, 2954-2965.

doi:10.1111/jan.13031

Kalmuk, G., & Acar, Z. (2015). The mediating role of organizational learning capability

on the relationship between innovation and firm's performance: A conceptual

framework. *Procedia - Social and Behavioral Sciences, 210*, 164-169.

doi:10.1016/j.sbspro.2015.11.355

Kaya, N. (2015). Corporate entrepreneurship, generic competitive strategies, and firm

performance in small and medium-sized enterprises. *Procedia Social and*

Behavioral Sciences, 207, 662-668. doi:10.1016/j.sbspro.2015.10.136

Kihn, L. & Ihantola, E. (2015). Approaches to validation and evaluation in qualitative

studies of management accounting. *Qualitative Research in Accounting &*

Management, 12, 230-255. doi:10.1109/QRAM-03-2013-0012

Kim, J. H (2016). *Understanding narrative inquiry: The crafting and analysis of stories*

as research. Thousand Oaks, CA: Sage.

Kornbluh, M. (2015). Combatting challenges to establishing trustworthiness in qualitative

research. *Qualitative Research in Psychology, 12*, 397-414.

doi:10.1080 /14780887.2015.1021941

Korstjens, I., & Moser, A. (2017). Series: Practical guidance to qualitative research. Part

4: Trustworthiness and publishing. *European Journal of General Practice, 24*,

120-124. doi:10.1080/13814788.2017.1375092

Krajnakova, E., Navikaite, A., & Navickas, V. (2015). Paradigm shift of small and medium-sized enterprises competitive advantage to management of customer satisfaction. *Engineering Economics, 26*, 327-332. doi:10.5755/j01.ee.26.3.6608

Kumar, V., & Pansari, A. (2016). Competitive advantage through engagement. *Journal of Marketing Research, 53,* 497-514. doi:10.1509/jmr.15.0044

Kwarteng, A., Dadzie, S. A., & Famiyeh, S. (2016). Sustainability and competitive advantage from a developing economy. *Journal of Global Responsibility, 7*, 110-125. doi:10.1108/jgr-02-2016-0003

Ladipo, P. K. A., Awoniyi, M. A., & Arebi, I. T. (2017). The influence of marketing intelligence on business competitive advantage (A study of Diamond Bank Plc). *Journal of Competitiveness, 9*(1), 51-71. doi:10.7441/joc.2017.01.04

Lancaster, K. (2016). Confidentiality, anonymity and power relations in elite interviewing: conducting qualitative policy research in a politicized domain. *International Journal of Social Research Methodology, 20*(1), 93-103. doi:10.1080/13645579.2015.1123555

Lau, A. K. W., & Lo, W. (2015). Regional innovation system, absorptive capacity and innovation performance: An empirical study. *Technological Forecasting and Social Change, 92*, 99-114. doi:10.1016/j.techfore.2014.11.005

Lee, V. H., Foo, A. T. L., Leong, L. Y., & Ooi, K. B. (2016). Can competitive advantage be achieved through knowledge management? A case study on SMEs. *Expert Systems with Applications, 65*, 136-151. doi:10.1016/j.eswa.2016.08.042

Lensges, M. L., Hollensbe, E. C., & Masterson, S. S. (2016). The human side of

    restructures: The role of shifting identification. *Journal of Management Inquiry,*

    25, 382-396. doi:10.1177/1056492616630140

Leung, L. (2015). Validity, reliability, and generalizability in qualitative research.

    Journal of Family Medicine and Primary Care, 4, 324-327.

    doi:10.4103/2249-4863.161306

Lev, B. (2017). Evaluating sustainable competitive advantage. *Journal of Applied*

    Corporate Finance, 29(2), 70-75. doi:10.1111/jacf.12234

Liao, T. S., Rice, J., & Lu, J. C. (2015). The vicissitudes of competitive advantage:

    Empirical evidence from Australian manufacturing SMEs. *Journal of Small*

    Business Management, 53, 469-481. doi:10.1111/jsbm.12078

Lis, A., & Sudolska, A. (2015). Absorptive capacity and its role for the company growth

    and competitive advantage: The case of Frauenthal Automotive Toruń company.

    Journal of Entrepreneurship, Management and Innovation, 11(4), 63-92.

    doi:10.7341/20151143

Liu, Y., & Liang, L. (2015). Evaluating and developing resource-based operations

    strategy for competitive advantage: An exploratory study of Finnish high-tech

    manufacturing industries. *International Journal of Production Research, 53*,

    1019-1037. doi:10.1080/00207543.2014.932936

Lub, V. (2015). Validity in qualitative evaluation. *International Journal of Qualitative*

    Methods, 14(5), 1-8. doi:10.1177/1609406915621406

Lusch, R. F., & Nambisan, S. (2015). Service innovation: A service-dominant logic perspective. *MIS Quarterly, 39*, 155-175. doi:10.25300/misq/2015/39.1.07

Lustgarten, S. D. (2015). Emerging ethical threats to client privacy in cloud communication and data storage. *Professional Psychology: Research and Practice, 46*, 154-160. doi:10.1037/pro0000018

Maharaj, N. (2016). Using field notes to facilitate critical reflection. *Reflective Practice, 17*, 114-124. doi:10.1080/14623943.2015.1134472

Mahdi, H.A., Abbas, M.K., Mazar, T.I., & George, S. (2015). A comparative analysis of strategies and business models of Nike, Inc. and Adidas group with special reference to competitive advantage in the context of a dynamic and competitive environment. *International Journal of Business Management and Economic Research, 6*, 167-177. Retrieved from http://www.ijbmer.com/

Makrakis, V., & Kostoulas-Makrakis, N. (2016). Bridging the qualitative-quantitative divide: Experiences from conducting a mixed methods evaluation in the RUCAS programme. *Evaluation and Program Planning, 54*, 144-151. doi:10.1016/j.evalprogplan.2015.07.008

Marshall, C., & Rossman, G. (2016). *Designing qualitative research* (6th ed.). Thousand Oaks, CA: Sage.

McCusker, K., & Gunaydin, S. (2015). Research using qualitative, quantitative or mixed methods and choice based on the research. *Perfusion, 30*, 537-542. doi:10.1177/0267659114559116

Menga, E., Dan, A., Lu, J., & Liu, X. (2015). Ranking alternative strategies by SWOT analysis in the framework of the axiomatic fuzzy set theory and the ER approach. *Journal of Intelligent & Fuzzy Systems, 28,* 1775-1784. doi:10.3233/IFS-141464

Miles, M. B., & Huberman, A. M. (1994). *Qualitative data analysis: An expanded sourcebook* (2nd ed.). Thousand Oaks, CA: Sage.

Miracle, V. A. (2016). The Belmont Report. *Dimensions of Critical Care Nursing, 35,* 223-228. doi:10.1097/dcc.0000000000000186

Mishra, C. S. (2017). Creating and sustaining competitive advantage. Cham, Switzerland: Palgrave Macmillan. doi:10.1007/978-3-319-54540-0

Mittal, S., & Dhar, R. L. (2015). Transformational leadership and employee creativity: Mediating role of creative self-efficacy and moderating role of knowledge sharing. *Management Decision, 53,* 894-910. doi:10.1108/MD-07-2014-0464

Mao, H., Liu, S., Zhang, J., & Deng, Z. (2016). Information technology resource, knowledge management capability, and competitive advantage: The moderating role of resource commitment. *International Journal of Information Management, 36,* 1062-1074. doi:10.1016/j.ijinfomgt.2016.07.001

Moczadlo, R. (2015). Creating Competitive Advantages - The European CSR - Strategy compared with Porter's and Kramer's shared value approach. *Ekonomski Vjesnik, 28,* 243-256. Retrieved from https://doaj.org/

Molina-Azorín, J. F., Tarí, J. J., Pereira-Moliner, J., López-Gamero, M. D., & Pertusa-Ortega, E. M. (2015). The effects of quality and environmental management on competitive advantage: A mixed methods study in the hotel industry. *Tourism*

Management, 50, 41-54. doi:10.1016/j.tourman.2015.01.008

Morse, J. M. (1994). *Critical issues in qualitative research methods*. Thousand Oaks,

CA: Sage.

Morse, J. M. (2015). "Data Were Saturated . ." *Qualitative Health Research, 25*, 587-588.

doi:10.1177/1049732315576699

Morse, J. M. (2017). *Essentials of qualitatively-driven mixed-method designs*. New York,

NY: Routledge.

Moustakas, C. (1994). *Phenomenological research methods*. Thousand Oaks, CA: Sage.

Mutunga, S., & Minja, D. (2014). Generic strategies employed by food and beverage

firms in Kenya and their effects on sustainable competitive advantage.

International Journal of Business and Management Review, *2*(6), 1-15. Retrieved

from http://www.eajournals.org

Neal, J. W., Neal, Z. P., VanDyke, E., & Kornbluh, M. (2014). Expediting the analysis of

qualitative data in evaluation. *American Journal of Evaluation, 36*, 118-132.

doi:10.1177/1098214014536601

Nelms, T. C. (2015). The problem of delimitation: Parataxis, bureaucracy, and Ecuador's

popular and solidarity economy. *Journal of the Royal Anthropological Institute,*

21, 106-126. doi:10.1111/1467-9655.12149

Ngah, R., Abd Wahab, I., & Salleh, Z. (2015). The sustainable competitive advantage of

Small and Medium Enterprises (SMEs) with intellectual capital, knowledge management and innovative intelligence: Building a conceptual framework. *Advanced Science Letters, 21,* 1325-1328. doi:10.1166/asl.2015.6018

Noble, H., & Smith, J. (2015). Issues of validity and reliability in qualitative research. *Evidence Based Nursing, 18*(2), 34-35. doi:10.1136/eb-2015-102054

Noorani, I. (2014). Service innovation and competitive advantage. *European Journal of Business and Innovation Research, 2*(1), 12-38. Retrieved from http://www.ea-journals.org/

Novak, A. (2014). Anonymity, confidentiality, privacy, and identity: The ties that bind and break in communication research. *Review of Communication, 14*(1), 36-48. doi:10.1080/15358593.2014.942351

O'Keeffe, J., Buytaert, W., Mijic, A., Brozović, N., & Sinha, R. (2016). The use of semistructured interviews for the characterisation of farmer irrigation practices. *Hydrology and Earth System Sciences, 20,* 1911-1924. doi:10.5194/hess-20-1911-2016

Oladokun, T., & Aluko, B. (2015). Corporate real estate strategies: The Nigerian experience. *Journal of Corporate Real Estate, 17,* 244-259. doi:10.1108/jcre-04-2015-0011

Oltmann, S. (2016). Qualitative interviews: A methodological discussion of the interviewer and respondent contexts. *Qualitative Social Research, 17*(2), 1-16. doi:10.17169/fqs-17.2.2551

Oxford Business Group. (2017). The Report: UAE: Dubai 2018. Retrieved from https://oxfordbusinessgroup.com/

Palinkas, L. A., Horwitz, S. M., Green, C. A., Wisdom, J. P., Duan, N., & Hoagwood, K. (2015). Purposeful sampling for qualitative data collection and analysis in mixed method implementation research. *Administration and Policy in Mental Health and Mental Health Services Research, 42*, 533-544. doi:10.1007/s10488-013-0528-y

Patton, M. Q. (2015). Qualitative research & evaluation methods: Integrating theory and practice (4th ed.). Thousand Oaks, CA: Sage.

Percy, W. H., Kostere, K., & Kostere, S. (2015). Generic qualitative research in psychology. *The Qualitative Report, 20(2),* 76-85. Retrieved from https://nsuworks.nova.edu/

Peticca-Harris, A., deGama, N., & Elias, S. R. S. T. A. (2016). A dynamic process model for finding informants and gaining access in qualitative research. *Organizational Research Methods, 19*, 376-401. doi:10.1177/1094428116629218

Porter, M. E. (1980). Competitive strategy: Techniques for analyzing industries and competitors. New York, NY: Free Press.

Prajogo, D. I. (2016). The strategic fit between innovation strategies and business environment in delivering business performance. *International Journal of Production Economics, 171*, 241-249. doi:10.1016/j.ijpe.2015.07.037

Pulaj, E., Kume, V., & Cipi, A. (2015). The impact of generic competitive strategies on organizational performance. The evidence from Albanian context. *European Scientific Journal, 11*, 273-284. Retrieved from http://eujournal.org/

Quick, D., & Choo, K. K. R. (2014). Google drive: Forensic analysis of data remnants. *Journal of Network and Computer Applications, 40*, 179-193.

doi:10.1016 /j.jnca.2013.09.016

Ranney, M. L., Meisel, Z. F., Choo, E. K., Garro, A. C., Sasson, C., & Morrow Guthrie, K. (2015). Interview-based qualitative research in emergency care part II: Data collection, analysis and results reporting. *Academic Emergency Medicine, 22,* 1103-1112. doi:10.1111/acem.12735

Ransbotham, S., Kiron, D., & Prentice, P. (2015). Minding the analytics gap. *MIT Sloan Management Review, 56*(3), 63-68. Retrieved from https://sloanreview.mit.edu/

Rashid, M., Caine, V., & Goez, H. (2015). The encounters and challenges of ethnography as a methodology in health research. *International Journal of Qualitative Methods, 14*(5), 1-16. doi:10.1177/1609406915621421

Ravanfar, M. M. (2015). Analyzing organizational structure based on 7s model of McKinsey. *International Journal of Academic Research in Business and Social Sciences, 5*(5), 43-55. doi:10.6007/ijarbss/v5-i5/1591

Reshidi, N., Hoxha, R., & Zuferi, R. (2015). Marketing strategies in the real estate industry in Prishtina. *Iliria International Review, 5*(1), 29-40. doi:10.21113/iir.v5i1.7

Robinson, O. C. (2014). Sampling in interview-based qualitative research: A theoretical and practical guide. *Qualitative Research in Psychology, 11,* 25-41. doi:10.1080/14780887.2013.801543

Rosciano, A. (2015). The effectiveness of mind mapping as an active learning strategy among associate degree nursing students. *Teaching and Learning in Nursing, 10*(2), 93-99. doi:10.1016/j.teln.2015.01.003

Rossetto, K. R. (2014). Qualitative research interviews: Assessing the therapeutic value and challenges. *Journal of Social and Personal Relationships, 31*, 482-489. doi:10.1177/0265407514522892

Roulston, K., & Shelton, S. A. (2015). Reconceptualizing bias in teaching qualitative research methods. *Qualitative Inquiry, 21*, 332-342. doi:10.1177 /1077800414563803

Roy, K., & Karna, A. (2015). Doing social good on a sustainable basis: Competitive advantage of social businesses. *Management Decision, 53*, 1355-1374. doi:10.1108/MD-09-2014-0561

Roy, K., Zvonkovic, A., Goldberg, A., Sharp, E., & LaRossa, R. (2015). Sampling richness and qualitative integrity: Challenges for research with families. *Journal of Marriage and Family, 77*, 243-260. doi:10.1111/jomf.12147

Saeidi, S. P., Sofian, S., Saeidi, P., Saeidi, S. P., & Saaeidi, S. A. (2015). How does corporate social responsibility contribute to firm financial performance? The mediating role of competitive advantage, reputation, and customer satisfaction. *Journal of Business Research, 68*, 341-350. doi:10.1016/j.jbusres.2014.06.024

Salavou, H. (2015). Competitive strategies and their shift to the future. *European Business Review, 27*(1), 80-99. doi:10.1108/EBR-04-2013-0073

Sarma, S.K. (2015). Qualitative research: Examining the misconceptions. *South Asian Journal of Management, 22*, 176-191. Retrieved from http://www.sajm-amdisa.org/

Saunders, M. N. K., Lewis, P., & Thornhill, A. (2015). *Research methods for business students* (7th ed.). Essex, England: Pearson Education Unlimited.

Schulz, S., & Flanigan, R. (2016). Developing competitive advantage using the triple bottom line: A conceptual framework. *Journal of Business & Industrial Marketing, 31*, 449-458. doi:10.1108/JBIM-08-2014-0150

Seo, Y. W., Chae, S. W., & Lee, K. C. (2015). The impact of absorptive capacity, exploration, and exploitation on individual creativity: Moderating effect of subjective well-being. *Computers in Human Behavior, 42*, 68-82. doi:10.1016/j.chb.2014.03.031

Siemińska E., & Krajewska, M. (2017). Conditions and directions of investing on the world real estate market. *Real Estate Management & Valuation, 25*, 99-112. doi:10.1515/remav2017-0033

Sigalas, C. (2015). Competitive advantage: The known unknown concept. *Management Decision, 53*, 2004-2016. doi:10.1108/MD-05-2015-0185

Sikora, D., Thompson, K., Russell, Z., & Ferris, G. (2016). Reimagining overqualified human resources to promote organizational effectiveness and competitive advantage. *Journal of Organizational Effectiveness: People and Performance, 3*(1), 23-42. doi:10.1108/JOEPP-03-2015-0012

Sitek, M. (2017). Innovativeness as a means to improve competitiveness in the real estate market. *Humanitas University's Research Papers Management, 18*, 161-173. doi:10.5604/01.3001.0010.2888

Smeets, J., Ploumen, T., & Meulenbroek, R. (2015). How to align the organization of the CREM-department to strategy during a recession. *22nd Annual European Real Estate Society Conference, 171-185*. doi:10.15396/eres2015_102

Solberg Søilen, K. (2015). A place for intelligence studies as a scientific discipline. *Journal of Intelligence Studies in Business*, 5(3), 35-46. Retrieved from https://ojs.hh.se/

Stahl, G. (2016). Relationship-building in research: Gendered identity construction in researcher-participant interaction. In Ward, M. (Ed). *Gender Identity and Research Relationships*, 145-165. doi:10.1108/s1042-319220160000014020

St. Pierre, E. A., & Jackson, A. Y. (2014). Qualitative data analysis after coding. *Qualitative Inquiry, 20*, 715-719. doi:10.1177/1077800414532435

Su, H.C., Linderman, K., Schroeder, R., & Van de Ven, A. (2014). A comparative case study of sustaining quality as a competitive advantage. *Journal of Operations Management, 32*, 429-445. doi:10.1016/j.jom.2014.09.003

Sugiono, A., Arifianti, R., Raharja, S. J., Maulina, E., & Hapsari, Y. D. (2017). Dynamic capabilities and creating organizational knowledge: Important linkage for building competitive advantage. *Russian Journal of Agricultural and Socio-Economic Sciences, 68*, 233-241. doi:10.18551/rjoas.2017-08.26

Sundarakani, B. (2017). Transforming Dubai Logistics Corridor into a Global Logistics Hub. *Asian Journal of Management Cases, 14*, 115-136. doi:10.1177/0972820117712303

Sutton, J., & Austin, Z. (2015). Qualitative research: Data Collection, analysis, and management. *The Canadian Journal of Hospital Pharmacy, 68*, 226-231. doi:10.4212/cjhp.v68i3.1456

Svarova, M., & Vrchota, J. (2014). Influence of competitive advantage on formulation business strategy. *Procedia Economics and Finance, 12*, 687-694. doi:10.1016/S2212-5671(14)00394-3

Tan, Q., & Sousa, C. (2015). Leveraging marketing capabilities into competitive advantage and export performance. *International Marketing Review, 32*(1), 78-102. doi:10.1108/IMR-12-2013-0279

Taneja, S., Pryor, M. G., & Hayek, M. (2016). Leaping innovation barriers to small business longevity. *Journal of Business Strategy, 37*(3), 44-51. doi:10.1108/jbs-12-2014-0145

Tavana, M., Zareinejad, M., Di Caprio, D., & Kaviani, M. A. (2016). An integrated intuitionistic fuzzy AHP and SWOT method for outsourcing reverse logistics. *Applied Soft Computing, 40*, 544-557. doi:10.1016/j.asoc.2015.12.005

Teh, D., & Corbitt, B. (2015). Building sustainability strategy in business. *Journal of Business Strategy, 36*(6), 39-46. doi:10.1108/jbs-08-2014-0099

Todericiu, R., & Stanit, A. (2015). Intellectual capital - The key for sustainable competitive advantage for the SME's sector. *Procedia Economics and Finance, 27*, 676-681. doi:10.1016/S2212-5671(15)01048-5

Vanpoucke, E., Vereecke, A., &Wetzels, M. (2014). Developing supplier integration capabilities for sustainable competitive advantage: A dynamic capabilities approach. *Journal of Operations Management, 32,* 446-461.

doi:10.1016/j.jom.2014.09.004

Virapongse, A., Brooks, S., Metcalf, E. C., Zedalis, M., Gosz, J., Kliskey, A., & Alessa,

L. (2016). A social-ecological systems approach for environmental management.

Journal of Environmental Management, 178, 83-91.

doi:10.1016/j.jenvman.2016.02.028

Vohra, V. (2014). Using the multiple case study design to decipher contextual leadership

behaviors in Indian organizations. *The Electronic Journal of Business Research*

Methods, 12, 54-65. Retrieved from www.ejbrm.com

Wamba, S. F., Gunasekaran, A., Akter, S., Ren, S. J., Dubey, R., & Childe, S. J. (2017).

Big data analytics and firm performance: Effects of dynamic capabilities. *Journal*

of Business Research, 70, 356-365. doi:10.1016/j.jbusres.2016.08.009

Wang, C. C., & Geale, S. K. (2015). The power of story: Narrative inquiry as a

methodology in nursing research. *International Journal of Nursing Sciences, 2,*

195-198. doi:10.1016/j.ijnss.2015.04.014

Wang, Q., Dou, J., & Jia, S. (2016). A meta-analytic review of corporate social

responsibility and corporate financial performance. *Business & Society, 55,* 1083-

1121. doi:10.1177/0007650315584317

Wargo, W.G. (2015). *Identifying assumptions and limitations for your dissertation.*

Menifee, CA: Academic Information Center.

Whipple, J. M., Wiedmer, R., & K. Boyer, K. (2015). A dyadic investigation of

collaborative competence, social capital, and performance in buyer-supplier

relationships. *Journal of Supply Chain Management, 51*(2), 3-21.
doi:10.1111/jscm.12071

Wicker, P., Soebbing, B. P., Feiler, S., & Breuer, C. (2015). The effect of Porter's generic
strategies on organisational problems of non-profit sports clubs. *European
Journal for Sport and Society, 12*, 281-307.
doi:10.1080/16138171.2015.11687967

Wiedmann, F., Salama, A., & Ibrahim, H. (2016). The impact of affordable housing
developments on sustainability in Gulf cities. *Open House International, 41*(4),
31-38. Retrieved from http://www.openhouse-int.com/

Workman, D., Kielhofner, G., & Taylor, R. (2017). Ensuring ethical research. In Taylor,
R. *Kielhofner's research in occupational therapy: Methods of inquiry for
enhancing practice* (2nd ed.), 144-161. Philadelphia, PA: FA Davis.

Yadav, P., Han, S., & Kim, H. (2016). Sustaining competitive advantage through
corporate environmental performance. *Business Strategy and the Environment,
26,* 345-357. doi:10.1002/bse.1921

Yazan, B. (2015). Three approaches to case study methods in education: Yin, Merriam,
and Stake. *The Qualitative Report, 20*, 134-152. Retrieved from
https://nsuworks.nova.edu/

Yin, R. K. (2014). *Case study research: Design and methods* (5th ed.). Thousand Oaks,
CA: Sage.

Yin, R. K. (2017). Case study research and applications: Design and methods. Los
Angeles, CA: Sage.

Zare, K., Mehri-Tekmeh, J., & Karimi, S. (2015). A SWOT framework for analyzing the electricity supply chain using an integrated AHP methodology combined with fuzzy-TOPSIS. *International Strategic Management Review, 3*(1-2), 66-80. doi:10.1016/j.ism.2015.07.001

Zehir, C., Can, E., & Karaboga, T. (2015). Linking entrepreneurial orientation to firm performance: the role of differentiation strategy and innovation performance. *Procedia Social and Behavioral Sciences, 210*, 358-367. doi:10.1016/j.sbspro.2015.11.381

Zivkovic, Z., Nikolic, D., Djordjevic, P., Mihajlovic, I., & Savic, M. (2015). Analytical network process in the framework of swot analysis for strategic decision making (Case study: Technical faculty in Bor, University of Belgrade, Serbia). *Acta Polytechnica Hungarica, 12*, 199-216. doi:10.12700/aph.12.7.2015.7.12

Appendix: Interview Protocol

Introduce the interview, research topic over coffee or lunch and explain the purpose and scope of the study. Assure the participants that I will keep all the collected information confidential, ask that I record the interview, and inform the participant of the right to stop the interview.

The questions for the interview are as follows:

Demographic Questions:

1. What is your age?

2. Where were you born?

3. What is your highest level of education?

4. How long in the current organization?

5. How many years of experience as a business leader?

Strategic Research Questions

1. What strategies do Dubai real estate business leaders use to attain and sustain competitive advantage to increase profitability during periods of unstable or declining markets?

2. How does strategic management or planning help you create and develop competitive advantage?

3. How do your strategies and business plans address the opportunities and threats pertaining to the changing economy and real estate industry of Dubai?

4. How does innovation contribute on attaining and sustaining competitive advantage?

5. What are the strategies you are generating as the UAE imposes a tax on 2018 affecting the real estate market?

6. How are you handling the current decline of Dubai's real estate sector with a falling rental and sales prices?

7. What additional information can you provide to help me understand strategies your organization uses to attain and sustain competitive advantage in changing real estate markets in Dubai?

Wrap up the interview by thanking the participant and schedule follow-up for member checking interview.

Follow-up and Member Checking Interview

Introduce follow-up interview and set the stage over coffee.

Share a copy of the succinct synthesis for each question and interpretation.

Ask a probing question related to any information that I found during the interview and related to the research topic.

Walkthrough, each question, read the interpretation and ask: Did I miss anything? Or, what would you like to add?

Wrap up the follow-up interview by thanking the participant.